Edited with an Introduction
by Ross C Murfin

Conrad Revisited

Essays for the Eighties

The University of Alabama Press

Library of Congress Cataloging in Publication Data

Main entry under title:

Conrad revisited.

   Outgrowth of an international Joseph Conrad
conference held at the University of Miami in
March, 1982.
   Includes index.
   Contents: Three problematical areas in Conrad
biography / by Frederick Karl — Heart of darkness
revisited / by J. Hillis Miller — Conrad's impressionism
and Watt's "delayed decoding" / by Bruce Johnson
— [etc.]
   I. Conrad, Joseph, 1857-1924—Criticism and
interpretation—Addresses, essays, lectures.
I. Murfin, Ross C
PR6005.O4Z58117   1985   823'.912   83-17937
ISBN 0-8173-0205-0

Conrad Revisited

To
Mrs. Blanka Rosenstiel
and the
American Institute of Polish Culture

Contents

Conrad Revisited

Ross C Murfin

Introduction:
Conrad in the Eighties

In March of 1982 the Department of English at the University of Miami hosted an international conference in honor of Joseph Conrad. The 1982 conference was the third to be held in Miami; like the 1974 and 1977 conferences it was made possible by the generous support of Mrs. Blanka Rosenstiel and the American Institute of Polish Culture. By the time the conference had ended with an al fresco reception at the Rosenstiel School of Marine and Atmospheric Sciences, however, there was a feeling in the air that something special, even extraordinary, had happened at the 1982 conference, a feeling stirred, perhaps, by the fact that seven hundred individuals had attended one or more of the lectures, a feeling borne out, now, by the publication of this important volume of essays.

Of the internationally known critics who came to Miami for the 1982 conference, only Frederick Karl, who had addressed both previous Miami meetings, was making a return trip. But it was far more than Miami that Karl was revisiting in 1982 and that he *is* revisiting in his essay entitled "Three Problematical Areas in Conrad Biography." It is also the world of Joseph Conrad, the question of biography in general, and—more specifically—his own biography of Conrad, en-

I

titled *Joseph Conrad: The Three Lives*. For in the last sentence of the revisionary essay published first in this volume, Karl suspects that, as for the number three, "it may be possible to multiply that several times over."

Karl is now implicitly questioning the biographer's effort to be accurate and complete. Returning to Conrad's life to find his examples, he builds a case for his emerging conviction that when biographers have sufficient data, they do not necessarily know how to use it, and that for some of the most important "facts" of a life there simply is no corroborating evidence. In the process of adding to what he told us in the 1979 biography, in the process of supplementing what we already "know" about Conrad's friendship with Gide, about his suicide attempt, and about his decision to write in English, Karl demonstrates the inadequacies of biographical method. He wonders why he uses available materials to make much of the Conrad-Gide relationship when other biographers have ignored it and still others—Gérard Jean-Aubrey, for instance—have chosen to use the materials so differently. He wonders why, unlike Baines and Berman and Meyer, he sees Conrad's suicide attempt as a form of self-resurrection. Finally, by way of a discussion of Conrad's decision to write in English, he concludes that the decision was only part of a larger cultural shift in Conrad, the etiology of which will probably remain a mystery forever.

The juxtaposition of Karl's revisionary essay on the biographer's dilemma and a provocative, poststructuralist reading by J. Hillis Miller of the novelist's most famous story might at first seem an odd pairing. Karl, the preeminent biographer, would presumably believe in the primary importance of authors who lived and wrote what they thought and felt and believed. Miller, the most prolific and influential American critic associated with so-called deconstruction, presumably questions the very myth inherent in the biographer's work with authors and focuses his critical attentions instead upon texts, texts which nonetheless cannot be called authoritative because they are against themselves, because their "revelations" contradict one another.

Like all the revisitations of Conrad published in this book, however, these two important essays reapproach Conrad in ways that, at times, run parallel. Karl's essay remakes the biographer into one who would interpret a life even as he admits that all biographies are interpretations and that interpretations, like Conrad's lives, are potentially and plausibly innumerable. Miller's revisit to *Heart of Darkness* (he first visited Conrad country in his 1960 book *Poets of Reality*) similarly remakes the critic, since Miller sees the well-known story as an illimitably interpretable text, much as are the parables of Jesus and the biblical book of Revelation, its generic anticipants. Interpretation becomes illimitable because the subject text, a parabolic apocalypse, is not itself a fixed and incisive interpretation or revelation. Indeed, Miller argues, the act of revealing or unveiling is always already an act of hiding and even of forestalling the revelation of that which is to be revealed, since what parables and apocalyptic texts invariably unveil is the act of unveiling itself, and this self-reflexive turning further obscures sight of that which is, therefore, always to be revealed.

Miller draws, in his essay, upon Jacques Derrida's recent writings, especially the essay entitled "Of an Apocalyptic Tone Recently Adopted in Philosophy." But the contexts of "*Heart of Darkness* Revisited" are not all French. Nor are they all poststructuralist in orientation. They include Ian Watt (whose recent discussion of *Heart of Darkness* in *Conrad in the Nineteenth Century* is said by Miller to be "the definitive placing of that novel in the historical context of the parabolic story"). They also include, of course, the chapter on Conrad in *Poets of Reality*, in which Miller discusses literature in which nihilism is exposed, and, eventually, transcended, in which Conrad is seen "prepar[ing] for the daylight of later literature."[1]

Bruce Johnson's critical tour de force, unlike Miller's, is entirely consistent in attitude — and critical method — with its author's earliest work on Conrad, in *Conrad's Models of Mind*, published in 1971. Still, Johnson's contribution to this volume offers something very new indeed, namely, the notion that impressionism probably belongs to a much broader and deeper epistemological shift during the late Victorian and early Edwardian periods than has as yet been recognized. Thus, although Johnson well knows that it is almost traditional to see Conrad as an impressionistic writer, he also revises tradition in believing that until impressionism is explained in terms of its broadest contexts and implications, and until texts such as *Heart of Darkness* and *The Secret Agent* are properly seen to share that turn-of-the-century phenomenological quest for "*epochē*," Conrad's impressionism will continue to be misunderstood and will, indeed, seem to place him among painters he neither liked nor comprehended.

The immediate context of Johnson's seminal essay is Ian Watt's recent book, *Conrad in the Nineteenth Century*. In that study, Watt uses a famous scene in *Heart of Darkness* — the one in which little sticks seen flying in the air turn out to be arrows — to show Conrad's dramatization of what Watt calls "delayed decoding," that is to say, the truthful interpretation of chaotic experiences by reason, the banishing of merely impressionistic experience. Using that scene and others (including the scene in *The Secret Agent*, almost equally famous, in which the sound of dripping blood is mistaken for that of a ticking clock), Johnson argues that Watt overvalues the act of decoding. He suggests that Conrad in fact was most interested in exploring the integrity of sensations unspoiled

4

by rational concepts and categories. Conrad is thus seen as an explorer much in sympathy with Husserl, for whom subjective impression—the *epochē*, or "bracketed" moment—was trustworthy and had the kind of presuppositionless eloquence that it had for a painter like Claude Monet.

Johnson, moreover, maintains that Watt, by rigorously delimiting his definition of impressionism in painting, has paradoxically made it more difficult to catch the philosophical spirit of the time and to understand that impressionism was far from delimited in turn-of-the-century consciousness. The most productive phenomenological approach to Conrad is thus, in Johnson's view, not through post—World War II literary critics like Gaston Bachelard or Wolfgang Iser. It is, rather, by way of a much more relaxed historical construction of the pre—World War I era, an era that had its beginnings with writers as various as Stephen Crane, Mark Twain, William James, and Charles Peirce and which produced not only Joseph Conrad and Edmund Husserl but also Gestalt psychology. Edward Said's pioneering phenomenology of Conrad's fiction, Johnson would argue, needs to be supplemented by an historical approach of the kind pioneered by Carl Shorske, an approach that will allow us to see both historical impressionism and early phenomenology as part of a larger cultural shift that has not yet been given a useful name.

Hunt Hawkins's contribution to this volume, a study with strong anthropological and sociological interest, might seem an unlikely piece to place next to Johnson's inquiry into the epistemological assumptions of an aesthetic movement. After some reflection, however, these two chapters come to seem, if anything, even more complementary than are the essays by Karl and Miller. Johnson has argued that Marlowe's undecoded impression of little sticks betokening no harmful intention, like the sensation in his feet of warmth and wet-

Ross C Murfin

ness, is left finally more trustworthy than the later, rational
deduction that a hostile attack has been planned and carried
out. From there it is really only a short step to the view
implicit in Hawkins's paper, namely, that imperialistic colonialism causes and is caused by interpretations of a foreign
world that are assumed to be rational but that in fact are
erroneous and harmful decodings of impressions that cannot
be decoded by Western assumptions.

Just as Hawkins takes political, anthropological, and sociological theorists—rather than literary critics—as his intellectual allies, so he sees Conrad as a writer going beyond the
notions of men like Herbert Spencer, St. George Mivart, and
Eduard von Hartmann and anticipating the ideas expressed
by Hannah Arendt, and, especially, by O. Mannoni (in his
famous study of the colonial situation, *Prospero and Caliban*). Conrad, like Mannoni, dramatizes the lives of men
living in a world without men, a world violently emptied out
by projective "interpretations" of native peoples and by the
decodings of their cultures that objectify both peoples and
cultures, rendering both subhuman. Thus Conrad's understanding has been sufficient to draw the praise of Third
World writers such as D. C. R. A. Goonetilleke, a Sri Lankan
quoted by Hawkins saying that Conrad's Malayan world is
"predominantly authentic," rendered without "conventional
Western prejudices."

If but a short intellectual step lies between Bruce Johnson's view of experience inaccurately decoded and Hunt
Hawkins's reading of the colonialist's (mis)reading of his
world, an even shorter step lies between Hawkins and Avrom
Fleishman. Fleishman in this volume develops his recent ideas
on landscapes and townscapes in literature by describing
several "landscapes of hysteria," one created by Stephen
Crane, one by D. M. Thomas (in *The White Hotel*), and
one—in *The Secret Agent*—by the writer Fleishman calls

6

"the grand master of the landscape of hysteria," Joseph Conrad. Whereas Hawkins pictures the colonialist alone in a world without men, a world dehumanized and even depopulated by his projections, Fleishman speaks of novels in which inward hysteria becomes the outward condition of the physical and political world. As Hawkins might, Fleishman wants to differentiate the novels he discusses from the novel of alienation as written by, say, Franz Kafka, whose works are characterized by a sense of the *disconnectedness* between characters and their environment.

Fleishman makes creative use of David Weimer, who coined the phrase "landscape of hysteria" to describe the fictional world of Stephen Crane. Like so many of the critics represented in this book, Fleishman revisits Conrad — revises our view of him — in part by placing Conrad's work in new contexts. This time those new contexts are neither those provided by anthropological theorists of the Third World nor the phenomenological writings that form the background of impressionism. Rather, they are those provided by the interpretive historians of nineteenth-century American literature, by Freud, and by a recent and shocking British novel that looks into the violence — military, psychological, and analytical — of man.

Whereas Fleishman, in mapping the trails of *The Secret Agent*, is revisiting territory that he has already explored in his book on *Conrad's Politics*, H. M. Daleski's essay on *Victory* is among other things an act of reparation. *Victory* is the major novel that Daleski ignored in his important 1977 book on Conrad entitled *Joseph Conrad: The Way of Dispossession*. In a letter written after the conference, he explains his earlier inattention to the book: "I didn't write on *Victory* for two reasons. I decided to discuss only what seemed to me to be first rate work, and followed Thomas Moser in delimiting that as falling between *The Nigger of the*

7

Ross C Murfin

'*Narcissus*' and *Under Western Eyes*. Furthermore, in my book I dealt primarily with the theme of self-possession. The question of self-possession in *Victory*," Daleski concludes, "seemed not to apply."

In recent years, however, Daleski has revised his own interests, and views, significantly. He has turned his attentions from Conrad to Dickens (in *Dickens and the Art of Analogy*), to Lawrence (in *The Forked Flame*), and, even more recently, to a subject that might seem a far cry from the one he explored in his Conrad book. Having once examined self-possessed heroes, he has in the past year published *The Divided Heroine: A Recurrent Pattern in Six English Novels*. It is precisely this new interest in self-division, however, that has led Daleski back to Conrad and to a revised estimate of the value of *Victory*, for it is as a divided, Victorian self that the protagonist of the novel, Heyst, now appears to Daleski, and it is through his self-division that, in Daleski's view, Heyst becomes a compelling character.

Daleski shares some of the emerging ideas about Conrad expressed by other contributors to this volume, but he also implicitly takes exception to some of his colleagues' views. Like Miller, he is fascinated by the contradictoriness of a novelistic world and of a character who is part of that world, but he suspects that "there is no need of a deconstructionist analysis to locate those contradictions that virtually thrust themselves at us." With Daniel Schwarz, whose contribution follows his in the volume, Daleski is coming back to the Conrad canon and valuing a later novel that he has come to see as undervalued, and yet he finds *Victory* of interest almost solely because of Conrad's splendid characterization of Heyst. Finally Daleski, like Robert Caserio, is revisionary in his attempt to reassert Conrad's connection with the great tradition of nineteenth-century *English* writers. (As Frederick Karl recognizes in the volume's first essay, "the pen-

8

dulum" in "recent years" has "swung toward stressing Polish influences: its literature, history, and general culture.")

Caserio, like Daleski, feels the strong presence of romance elements in the later novels. Those elements of escape and melodrama, in Daleski's view, serve at best as balances within a divided or dualistic world. (At worst, they are those elements that Conrad, when he succeeds, succeeds at rescuing his fiction from.) According to Caserio, however, those same romance story elements are what "rescue" Conrad's later fictions from the all-too-common claim that they are mediocre. In his provocative 1979 book on *Plot, Story and the Novel*, Caserio wrote as a partisan of romance, and it is clear from this new essay that he still does. Taking issue with critics from Virginia Woolf to Eloise Hay to David Thorburn—with those who have stated that in *The Rescue* Conrad's romance failed him and equally with those others who see romance as already failed mimesis—Caserio insists that *The Rescue* is a quintessential romance and that romance is quintessential representation.

A revolt against imperialism is the subject of *The Rescue*, and Caserio is as interested in the subjects of projective imperialism and the imperialism of projection as are Johnson, Hawkins, and Fleishman. Indeed, Caserio might be seen sharing an idea found in Johnson's paper, namely, the notion that the interpretation of some experiences as "savage" ones can in itself be the true act of savagery. And he would hardly argue with Hawkins's post-Mannonian reading of the colonialist. He would insist, however, that the adventure-filled, rescue-celebrating, literary form of romance is not one of the imperialistic conceptual nets that we must break through in order to see clearly and act generously. Its subjects, after all, are traditionally those who are righteously lawless; its principles are those of generosity; and its enemies are those who practice true imperialism, namely, those circumlocutions known to modern cultures, cultures that have lost sight of their own beginnings in the blood of righteous rebellion.

In opposing the views that *The Rescue* is a novelistic failure, Caserio comes specifically to oppose poststructuralist criticism, which he sees as in itself a form of imperialism. He suspects that deconstruction devalues romance precisely because it cannot admit the possibility of incisive representation that romance writers so ardently believe in. Poststructuralist critics are not unanalogous to colonial powers, Caserio suggests, because they believe that representative systems are like monetary ones, that is to say, fictive and arbitrary systems of exchange in which tokens of value are only tokens. Against such a view Conrad holds up not only an alternative view of representation but also the gift ring that is, in Caserio's view, representation's representation in *The Rescue*.

Daniel Schwarz, who since 1980 has addressed himself to the entire Conrad canon (*Conrad: "Almayer's Folly" to "Under Western Eyes"* was published in 1980 and followed in 1983 by *Conrad: The Later Fiction*) is allowed to have the last words in this volume. This is fitting, not only because his general essay balances the broad view of the author taken by Frederick Karl in the first essay, but also because in the process of defending his upwards reevaluation of the later fiction Schwarz articulates clearly certain ideas expressed, *sotto voce*, by two contributors who precede him in the volume, Daleski and Caserio. His essay takes issue, first, with the widely accepted view that the novels Conrad wrote after 1910 are markedly inferior to the earlier works. (First advanced by Thomas Moser in 1957, the argument received new impetus from Bernard Meyer in his 1967 psychoanalytic biography of Conrad.) Next, Schwarz takes issue with John A. Palmer, who reevaluates the later works, but who values them for their status as remote, symbolic, even allegorical works. Schwarz thus revises for the 1980s our outlook on the writer's canon: he is radical and revisionary enough to suggest that there is no radical or revisionary break in Conrad's canon or career, a career devoted to the exploration of human feelings, values, and self definitions. His revisitation of Conrad's world is thus interesting as well as believable, and because of that fact, too, his essay offers a fitting conclusion to this collective enterprise.

Frederick Karl

Three Problematical Areas
in Conrad Biography

All subjects, I am certain, make difficult demands on their biographers; but, I am equally certain, Conrad poses problems for his biographer that are special. There are areas in Conrad's life which are critical for our understanding of him and his work, and yet these very areas lack the necessary documentation or verification. Or else, in some instances, we have the necessary documentation but are faced with multiple decisions about its use. Thus there are two categories of problematical areas in Conrad biography: *first*, those areas which seem essential to an understanding of the subject, but for which we lack authoritative documentation; *second*, those areas for which we have documentation, but whose possibilities offer so many choices to the biographer that he can create several lives, not simply one.

In the first group, that for which we lack sufficient documentation, we may ask what Conrad was doing during the years he spent ashore. Of the twenty years he went to sea, almost half of that time was spent not on ships but ashore. Or, we may ask, what generated Conrad's decision to leave Poland just short of his seventeenth birthday? We have constructed a house of conjecture around this. Or, what were the factors in Conrad's decision to attempt suicide? We know of the deed, but almost nothing of his frame of mind in the days, weeks, and months before the attempt. In another context, what ingredients went into his choice of English as the language for his writing career? We have sporadic evidence, but it stops short of being conclusive or even satisfactory. Further, how did Conrad in his early and middle years feel about being a Pole? About the attacks directed upon him for his so-called desertion to English life and the English language? We have, once again, some documentation, but nothing definitive. Conrad eluded many of the crucial issues in his correspondence.

What really occurred in the relationship between Conrad and Marguerita Poradowska that led to the virtual silence in the correspondence after 1895? And if the correspondence did not end—we know there were letters—why were these letters suppressed or destroyed? We have convincing arguments, some of them psychologically based, but we lack sufficient hard information. To continue this first group, where we need documentation: how can we explain Conrad's shift from a sea career to a writing career, in a language twice removed from his native tongue? The shift of careers is itself difficult to explain, apart from the language involved. We can make all kinds of explanations and see the change of focus as a gradual, not an acute one, but nevertheless we are left with profound shadows and mysteries. Finally, for this same group of questions, how do we account for the leap that Conrad made between *The Nigger of the "Narcissus"* and his work of the next decade, beginning with *Heart of Darkness* and *Lord Jim*? His preface to *The Nigger of the "Narcissus"* is usually cited as the key document, but it really does not explain the leap; it explains, rather, how Conrad reached that particular point in 1897–98, not how he would go beyond it. In retrospect, it seems to us to have been the base for his further development, but it may not have been that at all.

When we turn to my second group, those problematical areas that result not from lack of documentation but from our difficulty with sifting through it to make biographical decisions, we have, once again, numerous examples. Some of these situations have to do with Conrad's relationships with other writers, which seem critical to his own stability and development. First of these is his association with Ford Madox Ford, the facts of which are solid enough, but whose interpretation has led in several directions: from Conrad's desire to apprentice himself to Ford in order to improve his English to a quasi-homoerotic attachment whose dissolution contributed to Conrad's severe nervous collapse. Another example could be Conrad's relationship with André Gide, a friendship maintained chiefly through correspondence. Gide directed a team of French translators of Conrad's work and, at the same time, offered to the older writer his earlier works, in translation, when Conrad could no longer write at that level of intensity. The association with Gide can be viewed in several ways. A third relationship we may cite is the one with his wife, Jessie. Although there is sufficient evidence to demonstrate that Conrad remained extremely devoted to her all his life—that the marriage was not an act of infantilism on his part but a shrewd, stabilizing move—nevertheless several commentators have viewed the marriage as lacking substance for Conrad, or as demonstrating his inability to confront real women in his life. Despite all the evidence of stability, the marriage has been given almost unlimited potentiality.

Still in this second group, where documentation is abundant, we have a slightly different kind of example: Conrad's illnesses, which began in childhood and recurred throughout his life in various forms, from physical ailments to ailments close to what Freud and his contemporaries were diagnosing as hysteria. It is possible to enumerate them, even identifying, incorrectly, I feel, an early phase as epilepsy, and then going on to cite malaria, gout, neuralgia, various psychosomatic attacks of one kind or another. Or else, the illnesses can be perceived as another form of infantilism, in which Conrad "played sick" whenever a situation became too difficult for him to face. But still another way is to see the illnesses as forms of preparation, as Conrad retreating into sickness and numbness to gather his forces for an artistic endeavor. We note this process with Virginia Woolf, and it may well apply to Conrad. But whatever decisions his biographer makes, he must confront quite varying interpretations of the same data.

Another example from this second group is the question of literary influences on Conrad, an enormous question in itself. In more recent years, the pendulum has swung toward stressing Polish influences: its literature, history, and general culture. That is all to the good, and yet Conrad himself stressed French literature, and we know that his reading while he was on board ships was heavily in English: Shakespeare, of course, but also Dickens, Cooper, Marryat, other English novelists, including George Eliot. The question of literary influences is a thorny one with all writers, since it involves areas of culture almost impossible to disentangle. Yet with Conrad, we have perhaps the most difficult case of all, spanning three cultures, three literatures, three languages. Also, in the background of his three languages was the presence of Russia, Prussia, and Austria: two more languages, three more cultures. In addition to literary influences, there were several other tremendous pressures on any writer-to-be: Darwin and Marx, Frazer and his ideas about primitive societies, Wagner and his primitive ideas about race and his sophisticated ideas about the arts, Ibsen's immense presence, issues concerning women and their rights. Conrad's imagination was prodded by an array of conflicting influences, some literary, some not: naturalism, symbolism, Polish, French, and English romanticism, or its remnants, the Wagnerian fever, the ambiguous realism of Flaubert, and so on.

My lists are at an end. If we reach into these episodes, we can construct biographically a Conrad of many coats, many colors, many tones. Put together in different ways, these elements can create a different Conrad for each biographer. Who is the real one? This is a valid question, for it poses an essential biographical query, which is, Does the biographer let his material lead him from one point to another without "imposing himself" on it, or does he begin with some thesis, which the life then illustrates? Or does he try to work somewhere in between? I believe that in this age of psychology biography can no longer be divested of its multiple meanings, which lie just outside of the documentation; the biographer is forced to work with theses, motifs, interpretations, analyses—as tastefully, we hope, as he or she can. He must create not only a life—although he must do that as accurately as possible—but also an understanding of it. He must have some biographical theory functioning in his life, whether it is an examination of the creative function, or an analysis of the writer in his culture. There must be integration as well as deconstruction, interpretation as well as adherence to data. Once this occurs, then biography becomes the sum of "everything," and the biographer finds himself with innumerable choices at every turn of his subject's life. We are now back to the beginning of my paper: those problematical decisions a biographer must make, even while he collects and sifts data for precise and detailed information.

I have selected three areas in Conrad's life to demonstrate how the biographer must "create" his subject's life even when he has a mine of information. My first example will derive from an association, that between Conrad and André Gide. At the second International Joseph Conrad Conference, held at the University of Miami in 1974, I presented a paper, which I later published in *Comparative Literature,* on the relationship between Conrad and Gide and how Gide introduced the older writer's work into the European literary scene. I established, then, the fact that the two met at least twice in Conrad's home in Capel House, near Ashford, Kent; that they corresponded for thirteen years, from 1911 until Conrad's death in 1924, with forty of their letters extant out of a possible fifty or more; that Gide supervised, along with Jean-Aubry, the translation into French of the entire body of Conrad's work; that Gide himself worked on the translation of *Typhoon* into French; that Gide dedicated his *Voyage to the Congo* "To the Memory of Joseph Conrad"; that, finally, Gide had used an epigraph from *Lord Jim* at the head of book 5 of *Lafcadio's Adventures.*

The lengthy correspondence and the interworking of Gide's career with Conrad's in his last decade are indisputable. We have documentation that establishes how touched Conrad was, initially, to find himself the focus of Gide's attention. We know of the extreme difficulties Gide underwent to make the translations possible, how he had to struggle against Conrad's attacks upon him for assigning women to the job, how he acceded to Conrad's demands for particular translators and even for modes of translation. Yet once we have cited all this, there are nagging questions for the biographer of Conrad. Despite all the evidence, he must find a pattern. Perhaps the most difficult of all decisions would be to assign the association and correspondence to Gide rather than Conrad biography.

Certainly Conrad's earlier biographers did that. Jean-Aubry, Conrad's close friend and a member of the Gide circle, while filling his biography with personal reminiscences, slighted the Conrad-Gide relationship and only briefly alluded to the correspondence. In a second biography, in which he attempted to update his earlier work, Jean-Aubry quoted from two letters but added little in this area. Conrad's other major biographer, Jocelyn Baines, refers only once to Conrad's association with Gide, quoting two lines from a marginal, published letter. If someone like Jean-Aubry who knew both parties intimately has chosen to see almost no significance in the relationship and correspondence, how can I justify my use? I thread the friendship through the final three hundred pages of my biography and make it an important event in Conrad's life, even as his creative powers were waning after *Victory* in 1914.

Let us enter the biographical process to see what possibilities exist. The difference in age between the correspondents—Conrad was twelve years older than Gide and well into his fifties—meant he was beyond any literary influence. Although Conrad was still middle aged, he was old in his feelings, his health, his sense of himself. With no clear influence as a guide, do we present such an association simply as an event; that is, it happened, certain documents support the occurrence, we produce the documents, and let it go at that? Or do we seek in material that might have meant more to Gide than to Conrad something that may have been of meaning to Conrad? If we do, we are leaving our documentation behind. It seems to me that in biography, as in psychoanalysis, everything has meaning; everything leads to some inclusion in the writer's thoughts and imagination, especially when another writer of considerable reputation offers homage. All such detail is of phenomenological importance. Yet this procedure means forsaking documentation and sailing out into foreign waters.

An interrelated question is, how much is permitted to the biographer who is concerned with a creative figure, with the growth of his or her imagination? Does anything go, in the sense that the subject's creative urge can lead to our unrestricted speculation about energy, talent, sources, one's use of those sources? What determines the limitations here, as the biographer moves into Freudian analysis, Jungian archetypes, Eriksonian stages of man, or other psychological tools, all of them imperfect and imprecise as ways of measuring the artistic imagination? I chose to make a good deal of the relationship between Conrad and Gide, although the letters between them with a few exceptions are not of top quality, although Conrad was himself beyond any direct influence from Gide or from the Continent, although the Conrad response was, in fact, mainly to Gide's choice of translators. My strategy was to "create" a scenario for the relationship and correspondence and then fit it into Conrad's life.

One of the perennial problems in Conrad biography is to explain the decline in his work. Some place it in 1910 after *Under Western Eyes*; I locate it qualitatively five years later, after *Victory* and *The Shadow-Line*. In either instance, there appears a recognizable decline in both creative strategies and language after 1915, in the final nine years of his life, beginning when he was still in middle age. Various explanations have been offered, from psychoanalytic interpretations based on Conrad's inability to confront the inner demons after his severe nervous collapse in early 1910, to others based on the war, on the fact that his older son was serving at the front, or to his own poor health and rapid aging. While all of these make sense, we are left with too many imponderables. I introduced the Gide association as a way of either decreasing the imponderables or, possibly, creating more.

When a writer's imagination begins to wane, especially when he is only in his early to mid-fifties, we sense wide gaps in our understanding of the phenomenon and we seek psychological explanations. I propose we can tackle the problem from the other end; that instead of seeking only reasons for the decline, we find reasons for Conrad's ability to keep going in those final years when inner voices were telling him his work was weakening; voices he acknowledged in letter after letter, including those to Gide. I chose to use the Conrad-Gide file as a way of demonstrating how Conrad held on, given the admiration and respect of Gide, given the translations which Gide promised, and given the particular tastes of Gide, which ran to early Conrad. I tried to account for Conrad's reimmersion in materials he had already put behind him, the manuscript of *The Rescue* being the most prominent; such materials reemerge under Gide's praise of his earlier career and Gide's work on translations, which brought back before Conrad the triumphs of his earliest years. I saw this circling back on Conrad's part as an aspect of the Gide influence—not Gide's own work, but the French writer's expressed tastes in Conrad's fiction and the translations themselves, which, as we have noted, offered up Conrad's early fiction for reexamination. In brief, Conrad saw his early career played back to him by way of the translations and by way of Gide's preferences, and he responded with the continuation of *The Rescue* manuscript and a series of novels which circled back to his earliest days, *The Arrow of Gold, The Rover,* the incomplete *Suspense.*

This is a curious use of material, and it may be biographically defective, since it makes a mockery of chronology and posits an imaginative thrust on Conrad's part which goes well beyond documentation, into the nature of creativity. I could have detailed the association with Gide in several other ways, of course: as, for instance, Conrad's need to associate with new friends after the split with Ford. Thus, Gide would become part of that second round of friends including Walpole, Jean-Aubry, Curle, Francis Warrington Dawson, replacing Wells, Garnett, Galsworthy, and the earlier group.

Another way was to ignore any creative or imaginative thrust and present the association as a straightforward event: Conrad delighted by Gide's interest, Gide paying homage to a writer he admired, their wrangling over the translations as an inevitable disagreement over business matters. A third way, as I mentioned above, was to see the relationship as belonging more to Gide biography than Conrad, since Gide was the initiator and the doer, Conrad the apparent passive element here.

Moving to my second example: a more fundamental episode in Conrad's life and one which has curiously not gained as much interpretation as it deserves is his suicide attempt, when he was twenty. There has been a book devoted to Conrad's exploration of suicide—Jeffrey Berman's *Joseph Conrad: Writing as Rescue*—but little effort to integrate the suicide attempt into Conrad's biography; that is, apart from the numerous suicides, near suicides, potential suicides which appear in his work, all charted by Baines, Meyer, Berman, and others. Jean-Aubry, of course, held to the duel theory, as did Jerry Allen after him. Baines established the fact of the suicide attempt, and to his credit dismissed once and for all the duel theory. But he was not interested in integrating it with Conrad's life, although he points to twelve actual or near suicides. Evidence for the attempt was first turned up as early as 1937 in a Warsaw journal and then when *The New York Times* published an article, "Conrad Once Sought to Take His Life." I am not concerned, however, with the establishment of the event. We can take it for granted. The significant element is what we make of it.

There are several coordinates here, many of them contradictory. Conrad insisted in *The Arrow of Gold* on the truth of his tale: that his fiction was absolutely true to life. But his retelling of early episodes there, with a love affair and duel as substitutes for the actual suicide attempt, is so full of inconsistencies, geographical impossibilities, anachronistic events, and romantic fantasies that we suspect Conrad indulged a family romance. Gun running with Dominic Cervoni, wild adventures and misadventures, the mistress of the Carlist Pretender, the wreck of the *Tremolino* are all run together at the time of the so-called duel, that is, the suicide attempt. Further, we have Bobrowski's letters to Conrad, which speak of gambling debts, of idling and drift, all intermixed; so that the suicide attempt is associated with a kind of Byronic existence whose authenticity is questionable. When Conrad presented it in the figure of Monsieur George, he overlaid events with so much romantic fantasy that fact and fiction cannot be distinguished. Further, according to Bobrowski's letter, Conrad extended an invitation to his creditor, Fecht, an act which suggests he wished to be found in a wounded condition; on the other hand, his attempt was a very real one. Putting a bullet through one's chest, near the heart, is not the same as taking pills and then calling one's doctor.

The possibilities for the biographer are unlimited. Suicide is such an act of desperation—even when it is not so final an effort as Conrad's—that we cannot disentangle it from the writer's imagination. It is part of his thinking even when he is not consciously thinking about it. I think *the least* of the importance of suicide in Conrad's life is the enumeration of suicides and near suicides in his work. These are significant but fail to penetrate the imagination. Far more significant is our attempt to establish what Conrad hoped to accomplish by his suicide, for he apparently intended to kill himself if he could not reestablish his life on different terms. We now enter very difficult terrain, for here the biographer is in the position I suggested above, of moving beyond his documentation into critical decisions with numerous possibilities.

Frederick Karl

The overriding motif in the suicide, I believe, was Conrad's attempt to remove himself from his uncle's dominance; it was an act of rebellion against someone who was smothering him with love, affection, money, and advice. His situation was, analogously, like that of Beethoven's nephew Karl, who also attempted suicide to escape from suffocating pressures. Intermixed with Conrad's so-called idleness, perhaps his sense of failure, his guilt about family prestige, was his uncle's criticism and his attacks on the paternal side of the family. There was on the uncle's part an effort to efface the father, Apollo, in the living Conrad, and since Apollo was for Conrad such an ambiguous force of good and ill we have a situation that can be broken up only by an act of extreme aggression.

If he cannot kill the uncle—shades of Hamlet!—then he will kill the uncle within him, which is to say himself. But whatever psychological interpretation we put on the act, it was one of termination: of a situation, a relationship, and even a life. Since Conrad did not attempt suicide again, as far as we know, this one-time effort indicates that he was not a "suicidal type," not a person who seeks in suicide a way out of every frustrating situation. His one effort, then, fits the pattern of someone cutting himself off; and even the invitation to Fecht can be perceived as a way of divorcing himself from his uncle. For Fecht was, as a liaison between Bobrowski and Conrad, an extension of the uncle; he was, further, a living example of everything that Conrad at twenty was not. If Conrad did indeed invite Fecht, Conrad's suicidal act was one of overwhelming aggression against Bobrowski. To contain the connection on its present terms, he would have to extirpate the uncle within himself.

Conrad's decision shortly after this to sail on English ships was based not only on his inability to obtain a French berth, but on a career choice which cut himself off even more dramatically. By leaving France, he left a country with strong historical ties to Poland; by moving to English ships and the English language, he was choosing neutral ground. His uncle would find it difficult to seek him there. What the biographer has wrought with his interpretation has, obviously, moved well beyond the documentation. Yet he has insisted on the primacy of a suicidal act in the conscious and unconscious perceptions of his subject. Conrad was a man of several dimensions, at least dualistic in some of his patterns, possibly more than that. He had established marginality as his mode when he chose to leave Poland just short of his seventeenth birthday, and the suicide effort must be perceived, I believe, as a need for marginality even if that decision led to self-destruction.

Conrad's self-will opened him up to a marginal existence which his uncle could not begin to comprehend, rational and balanced in his thinking as Bobrowski was. Conrad's inner life was turbulent, and I think it is necessary to see that suicide effort as central to that turbulence. When Conrad wrote about this episode in his life in *The Arrow of Gold* he could not project any intensity, and the reason why the prose fails is that he was being too duplicitous about his past, turning certain realities into fantasy, and then presenting the fantasy as truth. He was caught in contradictions between life and art, and art had to fail him since he could not admit the life. An admission of that life — in a work he called absolutely true — would have meant an intense entrance into his earlier years when even suicide was possible. I think *Lord Jim* makes a more telling impression of this episode, if we read the book as a shadow existence of Conrad's own journey.

Lord Jim, then, not *The Arrow of Gold*, is a closer analogy to Conrad's life during the period when he attempted suicide; if we seek coordinates for his desperate act, we can possibly find them here. Once again, however, the biographer has left his sources far behind in order to create coherence, or the semblance of it. With *Lord Jim*—both the novel and the character—Conrad indulged role playing; not only Marlow, but a whole series of roles through which he could locate himself in the text. He identifies with his idealistic subject and yet is capable of demonstrating that he is a bad citizen; he then shifts the terms, from Jim's absolute idealism, to those who argue relativism, and finds the latter, the relativists and those who forgive, far less noble than the man who has never learned moderation. Conrad scurries around Jim, seeking this pivot and that, this center or another, trying to discover the coordinates of his behavior. These responses by an author to the delinquencies of his character have their analogy in Conrad's correspondence with his uncle. There, Conrad is a Jim figure, and the uncle is the author trying to fathom from a distance what his delinquent nephew is up to. Yet as Conrad or Marlow moves closer to Jim, even establishing perimeters of behavior for him, he eludes them, slips through, as Conrad slipped through Bobrowski's advice to his own kind of triumph. Jim's desire to die, *his* suicide attempt, succeeds, the consequence of a miscalculation embedded in his own character; and Conrad shaves life that thin, like the bullet that passed through his chest and missed all vital organs. And just as Jim has moved outside anything that Marlow or Stein or the other commentators can comprehend, so Conrad moved beyond his uncle, freeing himself. With this interpretation, the biographer may also be attempting suicide.

Interpreting Conrad's suicide attempt, the biographer—unless he sticks to chronological and linear sequencing in his subject's life—moves into gray areas indeed. In my third example, we enter even deeper mists and fogs. We have documentation of a certain kind, but it is inadequate, and yet this third example is a real test for the biographer. I am speaking of Conrad's decision to write in English. Connected to this is the question of what impelled Conrad to write fiction at all, but this is too large a subject in present circumstances. It is, also, a subject with considerable documentation that leaves the biographer not much further along than when he started. The question of why Conrad decided to write in English rather than French, chiefly, or even Polish, is associated with the deepest reaches of his imagination and creative ability. Thus, to speak of this subject at all, we must leave behind biographical chronology and venture out. That nagging question arises: to what extent is this question part of biography, when its real answer lies in personal psychology where no exploration is satisfactory?

One way to look at the question is to say that Conrad was repeating the three languages of his father, Apollo, but reversing their use; so that the father's translating English classics into Polish becomes the son's transference of his Polish thoughts into English. Another, and not dissimilar, view is that his decision to sail on English ships was, in some related way, a decision to master the language of their sailors. Conrad himself spoke in *A Personal Record* of how English first came to him as a source of wonder and power when he heard it spoken by English engineers working on the Saint Gotthard Tunnel in Switzerland. Here, English is connected to a fairyland or mythical presence, for the men—practical and skillful—were involved with a huge hole in the earth; thus, English came to him as a kind of privileged moment, a revelatory experience. His first real exposure to the language outside of his father's translations was associated with the wonder of the circumstances in which he heard it. This "wonder," if we exploit it, becomes a biographical detail of some importance, but it is the biographer's construction as much as it is Conrad's.

In this connection, we could view the need to learn and

then write in English as somehow associated with the suicide attempt. That is, both are efforts to efface the past and to move on, to escape that part of his heritage which was destructive so that he could do his work. In this sense, the artist, here Conrad, is programmed at birth for certain work, and he must in his developmental stages find the means whereby he can accomplish it. This theory is very seductive for the biographer, since it removes the burden from him to prove something and places it on the subject. In this view, Conrad would expose himself to one difficult situation after another until he had escaped from enough of his past to be able to transform it into literature; his passage through ships and languages, then, would be a working out of destiny, like Aeneas and his vocation to found an empire.

Still another direction, and a profitable one, although also murky, is that Conrad tested out his kind of English as he wrote *Almayer* by writing a certain kind of French to Marguerita Poradowska. Here we enter thickets of possibility. In this sense, Conrad was trying out on Mme Poradowska, in French, the kind of language—florid, ornate, inflated, very much a language of end-of-the-century decadence—which he was attempting to use in his English novel. If we examine this idea, we see that Conrad's choice of English was a close thing, that it was associated with his knowledge of French, that it was, in fact, almost an English equivalent of French, allowing for the differences in idiom between the two languages. For the biographer, this view means that Conrad only barely edged over into English and had not made a real decision to write in that language, as he always asserted. He did say it was English or nothing for him as a creative writer, but if we see his English developing in the early 1890s, we can assert that he was so uncertain about its use that he had to try out some equivalent in French. Further, we know that Conrad hesitated and was interested in collaboration with his aunt;

so that language usage becomes blurred, not at all the clear decision he announced later.

In speaking of his life, Conrad almost always justified the way things turned out. He saw himself, in middle life, as having fulfilled a destiny—the breaking away, the sailing on French and English ships, the rise to a captaincy in the English maritime fleet, the turning to writing and the use of the English language. Conrad saw it all as this way and not any other. But for the biographer each of these decisions cannot be viewed as the hindsight of middle age. Each decision has within it a multitude of possibilities, and the career, as it is perceived from the outside, can obviously go in several directions. What the biographer does know—and here he can be certain—is that his subject turned out well; that each decision fitted into a mosaic of sorts, and the career worked. Or else, there would be no need for a biography. But those decisions that come at crucial moments in the subject's life cannot be trusted to what the subject says about them, even when *he* seems certain. The subject justifies his choice; but the biographer is trying to make sense of a life that was not linear and chronological, a life that moved as much in murk as in clarity.

Conrad's decision to use English, if we can even label it a decision as such, must be perceived as part of his entire shift from Poland to England. That is, like nearly every other biographical explanation of him, it must not be isolated as a detail; we must guide it toward the larger life, as part of the whole. Thus, all his explanations, while true in a limited way, are irrelevant as documentation since they explain *his* hindsight, not what really nourished his intention when the decision was made. English became unknown territory, although familiar as a written language in his father's study; and since Conrad was an explorer, a man profoundly fascinated by geography since childhood, we can posit that lan-

Frederick Karl

guage usage—in fact its very difficulties—was associated in his mind with exploration. We recall that Gide, caught up in the Conradian web of language, undertook the translation of *Typhoon,* whose maritime vocabulary was well beyond his command of English; but he, too, was an explorer, and language became part of that unknown territory which he would venture into.

I recognize that I have touched on issues that I cannot pretend to have settled in these brief remarks. I feel, however, that as new material surfaces and new biographies of Conrad are written, the latter cannot be simply a straightening out of the record. Conrad biography is something special, as I have attempted to show, for the material recovered is always outnumbered by great unknowns. We can marshal an immense amount of evidence, and yet the very things we wish to know recede even as we document our materials. I have, I hope, demonstrated that if I could call Conrad a man of three lives, it may be possible to multiply that several times over. Like Jim receding before Marlow's eyes, Conrad, to his biographer, recedes even as he becomes ever more immense.

J. Hillis Miller

Heart of Darkness Revisited

I begin with three questions: Is it a senseless
accident, result of the crude misinterpretation or gross transformation of the mass media, that the cinematic version of
Heart of Darkness is called *Apocalypse Now*, or is there
already something apocalyptic about Conrad's novel in itself? What are the distinctive features of an apocalyptic text?
How would we know when we had one in hand?

I shall approach an answer to these questions by the somewhat roundabout way of an assertion that if *Heart of Darkness* is perhaps only problematically apocalyptic, there can
be no doubt that it is parabolic. The distinctive feature of a
parable, whether sacred or secular, is the use of a realistic
story, a story in one way or another based firmly on what
Marx calls man's "real conditions of life, and his relations
with his kind,"[1] to express another reality or truth not
otherwise expressible. When the disciples ask Jesus why he
speaks to the multitudes in parables, he answers, "Therefore
speak I to them in parables: because they seeing see not;
and hearing they hear not, neither do they understand"
(Matthew 13:13). A little later Matthew tells the reader that
"without a parable spake he not unto them: That it might be
fulfilled which was spoken by the prophet, saying, I will

open my mouth in parables; I will utter things which have been kept secret from the foundation of the world" (Matthew 13:34–35). Those things which have been kept secret from the foundation of the world will not be revealed until they have been spoken in parable, that is, in terms which the multitude who lack spiritual seeing and hearing nevertheless see and hear, namely, the everyday details of their lives of fishing, farming, and domestic economy. Though the distinction cannot be held too rigorously, if allegory tends to be oriented toward the past, toward first things, and toward the repetition of first things across the gap of a temporal division, parable tends to be oriented toward the future, toward last things, toward the mysteries of the kingdom of heaven and how to get there. Parable tends to express what Paul at the end of Romans, in echo of Matthew, calls "the revelation of the mystery, which was kept secret since the world began, but now is made manifest" (Romans 16:25–26). Parable, one can see, has at least this in common with apocalypse: it too is an act of unveiling.

What might it mean to speak of *Heart of Darkness* as parabolic in form? Here it is necessary to turn again to that definition by the primary narrator of *Heart of Darkness* of the difference between Marlow's tales and the tales of ordinary seamen. This passage has often been commented on, quite recently, for example, by Ian Watt in his magisterial *Conrad in the Nineteenth Century*. Watt's discussion of *Heart of Darkness* seems also the definitive placing of that novel in the historical context of the parabolic story it tells. That context is nineteenth-century world-dominating European imperialism, specifically the conquest and exploitation of western Africa and the accompanying murder of large numbers of Africans. Watt's book, along with work by Frederick Karl, Norman Sherry, and other biographers, tells us all that is likely to be learned of Conrad's actual experience in the Congo, as well as of the historical originals of Kurtz, the particolored Harlequin-garbed Russian, and other characters in the novel. If parables are characteristically grounded in representations of realistic or historical truth, *Heart of Darkness* admirably fulfills this requirement of parable.

My contention is that *Heart of Darkness* fits, in its own way, the definitions of both parable and apocalypse, and that much illumination is shed on it by interpreting it in the light of these generic classifications. As Marlow says of his experience in the heart of darkness: "It was sombre enough, too — . . . not very clear either. No, not very clear. And yet it seemed to throw a kind of light."[2] A narrative that sheds light, that penetrates darkness, that clarifies and illuminates—this is one definition of that mode of discourse called apocalyptic, but it might also serve to define the work of criticism or interpretation. All criticism claims to be enlightenment, *Aufklärung.*

Conrad's narrator distinguishes between two different ways in which a narrative may be related to its meaning:

> The yarns of seamen have a direct simplicity, the whole meaning of which lies within the shell of a cracked nut. But Marlow was not typical (if his propensity to spin yarns be excepted), and to him the meaning of an episode was not inside like a kernel but outside [*MS:* outside in the unseen], enveloping the tale which brought it out only as a glow brings out a haze, in the likeness of one of those misty halos that sometimes are made visible by the spectral illumination of moonshine. (p. 5)

The narrator's distinction is made in terms of two figures, two versions of the relation of inside to outside, outside to inside. The hermeneutics of parable is presented here parabolically, according to a deep and unavoidable necessity. The meanings of the stories of most seamen, says the narrator, are inside the narration like the kernal of a cracked nut. I take it the narrator means the meanings of such stories are easily expressed, detachable from the stories and open to para-phrase in other terms, as when one draws an obvious moral: "Crime doesn't pay," or "Honesty is the best policy," or "The truth will out," or "Love conquers all." The figure of the cracked nut suggests that the story itself, its characters and narrative details,are the inedible shell which must be re-moved and discarded so the meaning of the story may be assimilated. This relation of the story to its meaning is a particular version of the relation of container to thing con-tained. The substitution of contained for container, in this case meaning for story, is one version of that figure called in classical rhetoric synecdoche, but this is a metonymic rather than a metaphorical synecdoche. The meaning is adjacent to the story, contained within it as nut within shell, but the meaning has no intrinsic similarity or kinship to the story. The same meaning could be expressed as well in other terms. Its relation to the story that contains it is purely extrinsic or contingent. The one happens to touch the other, as shell surrounds nut, or as shrine case its iconic image.

It is far otherwise with Marlow's stories. Their meaning is outside, not in. It envelops the tale rather than being en-veloped by it. The relation of container and thing contained is reversed. The meaning now contains the tale. Moreover, perhaps because of that enveloping containment, or perhaps for more obscure reasons, the relation of the tale to its meaning is no longer that of dissimilarity and contingency. The tale is the necessary agency of the bringing into the open or revelation of that particular meaning. It is not so much that the meaning is like the tale. It is not. But the tale is in preordained correspondence to or in resonance with the

34

meaning. The tale magically brings the "unseen" meaning out and makes it visible.

Conrad has the narrator express this subtle concept of parabolic narration according to the parabolic "likeness" of a certain atmospheric phenomenon. "Likeness": the word is a homonym of the German "Gleichnis." Both are terms for figure or parable. The meaning of a parable does not appear as such. It appears in the "spectral" "likeness" of the story that reveals it, or rather, it appears in the likeness of an exterior light surrounding the story, just as the narrator's theory of parable appears not as such but in the "likeness" of the figure he proposes. The figure is supposed to illuminate the reader, give him insight into that of which the figure is the phantasmal likeness. The figure does double duty, both as a figure for the way Marlow's stories express their meaning and as a figure for itself, so to speak, that is, as a figure for its own mode of working. This is according to a mind-twisting torsion of the figure back on itself that is a regular feature of such figures of figuration, parables of parable, or stories about storytelling. The figure both illuminates its own workings and at the same time obscures or undermines it, since a figure of a figure is an absurdity, or, as Wallace Stevens puts it, there is no such thing as a metaphor of a metaphor. What was the figurative vehicle of the first metaphor automatically becomes the literal tenor of the second metaphor.

Let us look more closely at the exact terms of the metaphor Conrad's narrator proposes. To Marlow, the narrator says, "the meaning of an episode was not inside like a kernel but outside, enveloping the tale which brought it out only as a glow brings out a haze, in the likeness of one of those spectral illuminations of moonshine." The first simile here ("as a glow") is doubled by a second, similitude of a similitude ("in the likeness of . . ."). The "haze" is there all around on a dark night, but, like the meaning of one of Marlow's tales, it is invisible, inaudible, intangible in itself, like the darkness, or like that "something great and invincible" Marlow is aware of in the African wilderness, something "like evil or truth, waiting patiently for the passing away of this fantastic invasion" (p. 23), or like the climactic name for that truth, the enveloping meaning of the tale, "the horror," those last words of Kurtz that seem all around in the gathering darkness when Marlow makes his visit to Kurtz's Intended and tells his lie: "The dusk was repeating them in a persistent whisper all around us, in a whisper that seemed to swell menacingly like the first whisper of a rising wind. 'The horror! The horror!'" (p. 79).

The working of Conrad's figure is much more complex than perhaps it at first appears, both in itself and in the context of the fine grain of the texture of language in *Heart of Darkness* as a whole, as well as in the context of the traditional complex of figures, narrative motifs, and concepts to which it somewhat obscurely alludes. The atmospheric phenomenon that Conrad uses as the vehicle of his parabolic metaphor is a perfectly real one, universally experienced. It is as referential and as widely known as the facts of farming Jesus uses in the parable of the sower. If you sow your seed on stony ground it will not be likely to sprout. An otherwise invisible mist or haze at night will show up as a halo around the moon. As in the case of Jesus' parable of the sower, Conrad uses his realistic and almost universally known facts as the means of expressing indirectly another truth less visible and less widely known, just as the narrative of *Heart of Darkness* as a whole is based on the facts of history and on the facts of Conrad's life but uses these to express something transhistorical and transpersonal, the evasive and elusive "truth" underlying both historical and personal experience.

Both Jesus' parable of the sower and Conrad's parable of

the moonshine in the mist, curiously enough, have to do with their own efficacy, that is, with the efficacy of parable. Both are posited on their own necessary failure. Jesus' parable of the sower will give more only to those who already have and will take away from those who have not even what they have. If you can understand the parable you do not need it. If you need it you cannot possibly understand it. You are stony ground on which the seed of the word falls unavailing. Your eyes and ears are closed, even though the function of parables is to open the eyes and ears of the multitude to the mysteries of the kingdom of heaven. In the same way, Conrad, in a famous passage in the preface to *The Nigger of the "Narcissus,"* tells his readers, "My task which I am trying to achieve is, by the power of the written word, to make you hear, to make you feel—it is, before all, to make you *see*." No reader of Conrad can doubt that he means to make the reader see not only the vivid facts of the story he tells but the evasive truth behind them, of which they are the obscure revelation, what Conrad calls, a bit beyond the famous phrase from the preface just quoted, "that glimpse of truth of which you have forgotten to ask." To see the facts, out there in the sunlight, is also to see the dark truth that lies behind them. All Conrad's work turns on this double paradox, first the paradox of the two senses of seeing, seeing as physical vision and seeing as seeing through, as penetrating to or unveiling the hidden invisible truth, and second the paradox of seeing the darkness in terms of the light. Nor can the careful reader of Conrad doubt that in Conrad's case too, as in the case of the Jesus of the parable of the sower, the goal of tearing the veil of familiarity from the world and making us *see* cannot be accomplished. If we see the darkness already we do not need *Heart of Darkness*. If we do not see it, reading *Heart of Darkness* or even hearing Marlow tell it will not help us. We shall remain among those who "seeing see not; and hearing

J. Hillis Miller

they hear not, neither do they understand." Marlow makes this clear in an extraordinary passage in *Heart of Darkness*, one of those places in which the reader is returned to the primary scene of narration on board the *Nellie*. Marlow is explaining the first lie he told for Kurtz, his prevarication misleading the bricklayer at the Central Station into believing he (Marlow) has great power back home:

> "I became in an instant as much of a pretence as the rest of the bewitched pilgrims. This simply because I had a notion it somehow would be of help to that Kurtz whom at the time I did not see—you understand. He was just a word for me. I did not see the man in the name any more than you do. Do you see him? Do you see the story? Do you see anything? It seems to me I am trying to tell you a dream—making a vain attempt, because no relation of a dream can convey the dream-sensation, that commingling of absurdity, surprise, and bewilderment in a tremor of struggling revolt, that notion of being captured by the incredible which is of the very essence of dreams . . ."
>
> He was silent for a while.
>
> ". . . No, it is impossible; it is impossible to convey the life-sensation of any given epoch of one's existence—that which makes its truth, its meaning—its subtle and penetrating essence. It is impossible. We live, as we dream—alone . . ."
>
> He paused again as if reflecting, then added:
>
> "Of course in this you fellows see more than I could then. You see me, whom you know . . ."
>
> It had become so pitch dark that we listeners could hardly see one another. For a long time already he, sitting apart, had been no more to us than a voice. There was not a word from anybody. The others might have been asleep, but I was awake. I listened, I listened on the watch for the sentence, for the word, that would give me the clue to the faint uneasiness inspired by this narrative that seemed to shape itself without human lips in the heavy night-air of the river. (pp. 27–28)

The denial of the possibility of making the reader see by means of literature is made here through a series of moves, each one ironically going beyond and undermining the one before.⌊When this passage is set against the one about the moonshine, the two together bring out into the open, like a halo in the mist, the way *Heart of Darkness* is posited on the impossibility of achieving its goal of revelation, or, to put this another way, the way it is a revelation of the impossibility of revelation.⌉

In Conrad's parable of the moonshine, the moon shines already with reflected and secondary light. Its light is reflected from the primary light of that sun which is almost never mentioned as such in *Heart of Darkness*. The sun is only present in the glitter of its reflection from this or that object, for example, the surface of that river which, like the white place of the unexplored Congo on the map, fascinates Marlow like a snake. In one passage it is moonlight, already reflected light, which is reflected again from the river: "The moon had spread over everything a thin layer of silver—over the rank grass, over the mud, upon the wall of matted vegetation standing higher than the wall of a temple, over the great river I could see through a sombre gap glittering, glittering, as it flowed broadly by without a murmur" (p. 27). In the case of the parable of the moonshine too that halo brought out in the mist is twice-reflected light. The story, according to Conrad's analogy, the facts that may be named and seen, is the moonlight, while the halo brought out around the moon by the reflection of the moonlight from the diffused, otherwise invisible droplets of the mist, is the meaning of the tale, or rather, the meaning of the tale is the darkness which is made visible by that halo of twice-reflected light. But of course the halo does nothing of the sort. It only makes visible more light. What can be seen is only what can be seen. In the end this is always only more light, direct or reflected. The darkness is in principle invisible and remains invisible. All that can be said is that the halo gives the spectator indirect knowledge that the darkness is there. The glow brings out the haze, the story brings out its meaning, by magically generating knowledge that something is there, the haze in one case, the meaning of the story, inarticulate and impossible to be articulated, in any direct way at least, in the other. The expression of the meaning of the story is never the plain statement of that meaning but is always no more than a parabolic "likeness" of the meaning, as the haze is brought out "in the likeness of one of those misty halos that sometimes are made visible by the spectral illumination of moonshine."

In the passage in which Marlow makes explicit his sense of the impossibility of his enterprise he says to his auditors on the *Nellie* first that he did not see Kurtz in his name any more than they do. The auditors of any story are forced to see everything of the story "in its name," since a story is made of nothing but names and their adjacent words. There is nothing to see literally in any story except the words on the page, the movement of the lips of the teller. Unlike Marlow, his listeners never have a chance to see or experience directly the man behind the name. The reader, if he happens at this moment to think of it (and the passage is clearly an invitation to such thinking, an invocation of it), is in exactly the same situation as that of Marlow's auditors, only worse. When Marlow appeals to his auditors Conrad is by a kind of ventriloquism appealing to his readers: "Do you see him? Do you see the story? Do you see anything? It seems to me I am trying to tell you a dream—making a vain attempt." Conrad speaks through Marlow to us. The reader too can reach the truth behind the story only through names, never through any direct perception or experience. In the reader's case it is not even names proffered by a living man before him, only names coldly and impersonally printed on the pages of the book he holds in his hand. Even if the reader goes behind the fiction to the historical reality on which it is based, as Ian Watt and others have done, he or she will only confront more words on more pages, Conrad's letters or the historical records of the conquest and exploitation of the Congo. The situation of the auditors even of a living speaker, Marlow says, is scarcely better, since what a story must convey through names and other words is not the fact but the "life-sensation" behind the fact "which makes its truth, its meaning—its subtle and penetrating essence." This is once more the halo around the moon, the meaning enveloping the tale. This meaning is as impossible to convey by way of the life-facts that may be named as the "dream-sensation" is able to be conveyed through a relation of the bare facts of the dream. Anyone knows this who has ever tried to tell another person his dream and has found how lame and flat, or how laughable, it sounds, since "no relation of a dream can convey the dream-sensation." According to Marlow's metaphor or proportional analogy: as the facts of a dream are to the "dream-sensation," so the facts of a life are to the "life-sensation." Conrad makes an absolute distinction between experience and the interpretation of written or spoken signs. The sensation may only be experienced directly and may by no means, oral or written, be communicated to another: "We live, as we dream, alone."

Nevertheless, Marlow tells his auditors, they have one direct or experimental access to the truth enveloping the story: "You fellows see more than I could then. You see me, whom you know." There is a double or even triple irony in this. To see the man who has had the experience is to have an avenue to the experience for which the man speaks, to which he bears witness. Marlow's auditors see more than he could then, that is, before his actual encounter with Kurtz. Ironically, the witness cannot bear witness for himself. He cannot see himself or cannot see through himself or by means of himself, in spite of, or in contradiction of, Conrad's (or Marlow's) assertion a few paragraphs later that work is "the chance to find yourself. Your own reality—for yourself, not for others—what no other man can ever know. They can only see the mere show, and never can tell what it really means" (p. 29). Though each man can only experience his own reality, his own truth, the paradox involved here seems to run, he can only experience it through another or by means of another as witness to a truth deeper in, behind the other. Marlow's auditors can only learn indirectly, through Marlow, whom they see. They therefore know more than he did. Marlow could only learn through Kurtz, when he finally encountered him face to face. The reader of *Heart of Darkness* learns through the relation of the primary narrator, who learned through Marlow, who learned through Kurtz. This proliferating relay of witnesses, one behind another, each revealing another truth further in which turns out to be only another witness corresponds to the narrative form of *Heart of Darkness*. The novel is a sequence of episodes, each structured according to the model of appearances, signs, which are also obstacles or veils. Each veil must be lifted to reveal a truth behind which always turns out to be another episode, another witness, another veil to be lifted in its turn. Each such episode is a "fact dazzling, to be seen, like the foam on the depths of the sea, like a ripple on an unfathomable enigma" (p. 43), the fact for example that though the cannibal Africans on Marlow's steamer were starving, they did not eat the white men. But behind each enigmatic fact is only another fact. The relay of witness behind witness behind witness, voice behind voice behind voice, each speaking in ventriloquism through the one next farther out, is a genre of the apocalypse. The book of Revelation, in the Bible, is the paradigmatic example in our tradition, though of course it is by no means the only example. In Revelation God speaks through Jesus, who speaks through a messenger angel, who speaks through John of Patmos, who speaks to us.

There is another reason beyond the necessities of revelation for this structure. The truth behind the last witness, behind Kurtz for example in *Heart of Darkness,* is, no one can doubt it, death, "the horror"; or, to put this another way, "death" is another name for what Kurtz names "the horror." No man can confront that truth face to face and survive. Death or the horror can only be experienced indirectly, by way of the face and voice of another. The relay of witnesses both reveals death and, luckily, hides it. As Marlow says, "the inner truth is hidden—luckily, luckily" (p. 34). This is another regular feature of the genre of the apocalypse. The word apocalypse means "unveiling," "revelation," but what the apocalypse unveils is not the truth of the end of the world which it announces, but the act of unveiling. The unveiling unveils unveiling. It leaves its readers, auditors, witnesses, as far as ever from the always not quite yet of the imminent revelation—luckily. Marlow says it was not his own near-death on the way home down the river, "not my own extremity I remember best," but Kurtz's "extremity that I seem to have lived through." Then he adds, "True, he had made that last stride, he had stepped over the edge, while I had been permitted to draw back my hesitating foot. And perhaps this is the whole difference; perhaps all the wisdom, and all truth, and all sincerity, are just compressed into that inappreciable moment of time in which we step over the threshold of the invisible. Perhaps!" (p. 72). Marlow, like Orpheus returning without Eurydice from the land of the dead, comes back to civilization with nothing, nothing to witness to, nothing to reveal but the process of unveiling that makes up the whole of the narration of *Heart of Darkness.* Marlow did not go far enough into the darkness, but if he had, like Kurtz he could not have come back. All the reader gets is Marlow's report of

Kurtz's last words, that and a description of the look on Kurtz's face: "It was as though a veil had been rent. I saw on that ivory face the expression of sombre pride, of ruthless power, of craven terror—of an intense and hopeless despair" (pp. 70–71).

I have said there is a triple irony in what Marlow says when he breaks his narration to address his auditors directly. If the first irony is the fact that the auditors see more than Marlow did because they see Marlow, whom they know, or as Conrad elsewhere puts this, "the onlookers see most of the game," the second irony is that we readers of the novel, if we happen to think at this moment of our own situation, realize that we must therefore see nothing. We see and can see no living witness, not the primary narrator, not Marlow, not Kurtz, not even Conrad himself, who is now only a voice from the dead for us. We see only the lifeless words on the page, the names Marlow, Kurtz, and so on, Conrad's name on the title page. By Marlow's own account that is not enough. Seeing only happens by direct experience, and no act of reading is direct experience. The book's claim to give the reader access to the dark truth behind appearance is withdrawn by the terms in which it is proffered.

The third irony in this relay of ironies behind ironies is that Marlow's auditors of course do not see Marlow either. It is too dark. They hear only his disembodied voice. "It had become so pitch dark," says the narrator, "that we listeners could hardly see one another. For a long time already he, sitting apart, had been no more to us than a voice." Marlow's narrative does not seem to be spoken by a living incarnate witness, there before his auditors in the flesh. It is a "narrative that seemed to shape itself without human lips in the heavy night-air of the river." This voice can be linked to no individual speaker or writer as the ultimate source of its message, not to Marlow, nor to Kurtz, nor to the first narrator, nor even to Conrad himself. The voice is spoken by no one to no one. It always comes from another, from the other of any identifiable speaker or writer. It traverses all these voices as what speaks through them. It gives them authority and at the time dispossesses them, deprives them of authority, since they only speak with the delegated authority of another. As Marlow says of the voice of Kurtz and of all the other voices, they are what remain as a dying unanimous and anonymous drone or clang that exceeds any single identifiable voice and in the end is spoken by no one: "A voice. He was very little more than a voice. And I heard him—it—this voice—other voices—all of them were so little more than voices—and the memory of that time itself lingers around me, impalpable, like a dying vibration of one immense jabber, silly, atrocious, sordid, savage, or simply mean, without any kind of sense, Voices, voices— . . ."(p. 49).

For the reader too *Heart of Darkness* lingers in the mind or memory chiefly as a cacophony of dissonant voices. It is as though the story were spoken or written not by an identifiable narrator but directly by the darkness itself, just as Kurtz's last words seem whispered by the circumambient dusky air when Marlow makes his visit to Kurtz's Intended, and just as Kurtz himself presents himself to Marlow as a voice, a voice which exceeds Kurtz and seems to speak from beyond him: "Kurtz discoursed. A voice! a voice! It rang deep to the very last. It survived his strength to hide in the magnificent folds of eloquence the barren darkness of his heart" (p. 69). Kurtz has "the gift of expression, the bewildering, the illuminating, the most exalted and the most contemptible, the pulsating stream of light, or the deceitful flow from the heart of an impenetrable darkness" (p. 48). Kurtz has intended to use his eloquence as a means of "wringing the heart of the wilderness," but "the wilderness had found him out early, and had taken on him a terrible vengeance for the fantastic invasion"

(p. 59). The direction of the flow of language reverses. It flows from the darkness instead of toward it. Kurtz is "hollow at the core" (p. 59), and so the wilderness can speak through him, use him so to speak as a ventriloquist's dummy through which its terrible messages may be broadcast to the world: "Exterminate all the brutes!" "the horror!" (pp. 51, 71). The speaker to is spoken through. Kurtz's disembodied voice, or the voice behind voice behind voice of the narrators, or that "roaring chorus of articulated, rapid, breathless utterance" (p. 68) shouted by the natives on the bank, when Kurtz is taken on board the steamer—these are in the end no more direct a testimony of the truth than the words on the page as Conrad wrote them. The absence of a visible speaker of Marlow's words and the emphasis on the way Kurtz is a disembodied voice function as indirect expressions of the fact that *Heart of Darkness* itself is words without person, words which cannot be traced back to any single personality. This is once more confirmation of my claim that *Heart of Darkness* belongs to the genre of the apocalypse. This novel is an apocalyptic parable or a parabolic apocalypse. The apocalypse is after all a written not an oral genre, and it turns on the "Come" spoken or written always by someone other than the one who seems to utter or write it.[3]

A full exploration of the way *Heart of Darkness* is an apocalypse would need to be put under the multiple aegis of the converging figures of irony, antithesis, catachresis, synecdoche, aletheia, and prosopopoeia. Irony is a name for the pervasive tone of Marlow's narration, which undercuts as it affirms. Antithesis identifies the division of what is presented in the story in terms of seemingly firm oppositions which always ultimately break down. Catachresis is the proper name for a parabolic revelation of the darkness by means of visible figures that do not substitute for any possible literal expression of that darkness. Synecdoche is the name for the questionable relation of similarity between the visible sign, the skin of the surface, the foam on the sea, and what lies behind it, the pulsating heart of darkness, the black depths of the sea. Unveiling or *aletheia* labels that endless process of apocalyptic revelation which never quite comes off. The revelation is always future. We must always go on watching and waiting for it, as the primary narrator remains wakeful, on the watch for the decisive clue in Marlow's narration. Personification, finally, is a name for the consistent presentation of the darkness in terms of the trope prosopopoeia. The reader encounters the darkness always as some kind of living creature with a heart, ultimately as a woman who unmans all those male questors who try to dominate her. This pervasive personification is more dramatically embodied in the native woman, Kurtz's mistress: "the immense wilderness, the colossal body of the fecund and mysterious life seemed to look at her, pensive, as though it had been looking at the image of its own tenebrous and passionate soul" (p. 62).

Heart of Darkness is perhaps most explicitly apocalyptic in announcing the end, the end of Western civilization, or of Western imperialism, the reversal of idealism into savagery. As is always the case with apocalypses, the end is announced as something always imminent, never quite yet. Apocalypse is never now. The novel sets women, who are out of it, against men, who can live with the facts and have a belief to protect them against the darkness. Men can breathe dead hippo and not be contaminated. Male practicality and idealism reverse, however. They turn into their opposites because they are hollow at the core. They are vulnerable to the horror. They *are* the horror. The idealistic suppression of savage customs becomes, "Exterminate all the brutes!" Male idealism is the same thing as the extermination of the brutes. The suppression of savage customs is the extermination of the brutes. This is not just wordplay but actual fact, as the history of the white man's conquest of the world has abundantly demonstrated. This conquest means the end of the brutes, but it means also, in Conrad's view of history, the end of Western civilization, with its ideals of progress, enlightenment, and reason, its goal of carrying the torch of civilization into the wilderness and wringing the heart of the darkness. Or it is the imminence of that end which has never quite come as long as there is someone to speak or write of it.

I claim to have demonstrated that *Heart of Darkness* is not only parabolic but also apocalyptic. It fits that strange genre of the apocalyptic text, the sort of text that promises an ultimate revelation without giving it, and says always "Come" and "Wait." But there is an extra twist given to the paradigmatic form of the apocalypse in *Heart of Darkness*. The *Aufklärung* or enlightenment in this case is of the fact that the darkness can never be enlightened. The darkness enters into every gesture of enlightenment to enfeeble it, to hollow it out, to corrupt it and thereby to turn its reason into unreason, its pretense of shedding light into more darkness. Marlow as narrator is in complicity with this reversal in the act of identifying it in others. He too claims, like the characteristic writer of an apocalypse, to know something no one else knows and to be qualified on that basis to judge and enlighten them. "I found myself back in the sepulchral city," says Marlow of his return from the Congo, "resenting the sight of people hurrying through the streets to filch a little money from each other, to devour their infamous cookery, to gulp their unwholesome beer, to dream their insignificant and silly dreams. They trespassed upon my thoughts. They were intruders whose knowledge of life was to me an irritating pretense because I felt so sure they could not possibly know the things I knew" (p. 72).

The consistent tone of Marlow's narration is ironical. Irony is truth telling or a means of truth telling, of unveiling.

At the same time it is a defense against the truth. This doubleness makes it, though it seems so coolly reasonable, another mode of unreason, the unreason of a fundamental undecidability. If irony is a defense, it is also inadvertently a means of participation. Though Marlow says, "I have a voice too, and for good or evil mine is the speech that cannot be silenced" (p. 37), as though his speaking were a cloak against the darkness, he too, in speaking ironically, becomes, like Kurtz, one of those speaking tubes or relay stations through whom the darkness speaks. As theorists of irony from Friedrich Schlegel and Søren Kierkegaard to Paul de Man have argued, irony is the one trope that cannot be mastered or used as an instrument of mastery. Any ironic statement is essentially indeterminate or undecidable in meaning. The man who attempts to say one thing while clearly meaning another ends up by saying the first thing too, in spite of himself. One irony leads to another. The ironies proliferate into a great crowd of little conflicting ironies. It is impossible to know in just what tone of voice one should read one of Marlow's sardonic ironies. Each is uttered simultaneously in innumerable conflicting tones going all the way from the lightest and most comical to the darkest, most somber and tragic. It is impossible to decide exactly which quality of voice should be allowed to predominate over the others. Try reading a given passage aloud and you will see this. Marlow's description of the clamor of native voices on the shore or of the murmur of all those voices he remembers from that time in his life also functions as an appropriate displaced description of the indeterminations of tone and meaning in his own discourse. Marlow's irony makes his speech in its own way another version of that multiple cacophonous and deceitful voice flowing from the heart of darkness, "a complaining clamour, modulated in savage discords," or a "tumultuous and mournful uproar," another version of that "one immense

J. Hillis Miller

jabber, silly, atrocious, sordid, savage, or simply mean, without any kind of sense," not a voice, but "voices" (pp. 40, 49). In this inextricable tangle of voices and voices speaking within voices, Marlow's narration fulfills, no doubt without deliberate intent on Conrad's part, one of the primary laws of the genre of the apocalypse.

The final fold in this folding in of complicities in these ambiguous acts of unveiling is my own complicity as demystifying commentator. Behind or before Marlow is Conrad, and before or behind him stands the reader or critic. My commentary unveils a lack of decisive unveiling in *Heart of Darkness*. I have attempted to perform an act of generic classification, with all the covert violence and unreason of that act, since no work is wholly commensurate with the boundaries of any genre. By unveiling the lack of unveiling in *Heart of Darkness*, I have become another witness in my turn, as much guilty as any other in the line of witnesses of covering over while claiming to illuminate. My *Aufklärung* too has been of the continuing impenetrability of Conrad's *Heart of Darkness*.

Bruce Johnson

Conrad's Impressionism and Watt's "Delayed Decoding"

Ian Watt's careful probing of Conrad's "impressionism" in *Conrad in the Nineteenth Century,* despite its canny ability to capture the flavor of time and place, leads us nonetheless to slight one of historic impressionism's most important aspects: the participation of so many of these artists—including Conrad—in the original Lockean sense of both the word *impressionism* and the extended epistemology it implies.[1] Popular art history usually asserts that instead of painting a tree, the impressionist painted the effect of a tree on a particular sensibility; Lewis Mumford somewhere uses just that phrase, "the effect of a tree," to note impressionism's shift from object to affect. In the same historical shorthand, expressionism then becomes the objectification of powerful emotions emerging from that now no-longer-screening but originating sensibility. In Stephen Crane we can sometimes see the entire process in a single sentence.

Joseph Conrad, however, saw even in his first two novels that for the writer as for the painter there could be no such bald act as "painting a tree." As E. H. Gombrich and other art historians have shown, the aesthetic tradition and its models largely determine how a tree or anything else is represented. Albrecht Dürer's strange woodcut of a largely imagined rhinoceros is decisive for other artists even after they have seen the real thing in Africa two hundred years later.[2] The painter who attempts "objectively" to "paint a tree" at least begins with what his culture and his aesthetic traditions prepare him and allow him to see. There is in short no easy, "realist" alternative to impressionism; the impressionist, as Conrad apparently understood the term, seeks not only to render "the effect of a tree," with all the emotional and visual peculiarities of the individual point of view, but to remind the reader continually that what he might easily and readily assume to be "objectively" the tree is actually the result of complex cultural prejudices. And those preconceptions, he knew, work in the viewer and reader even less obviously than the unique personal peculiarities of his point of view. We can agree that in matters of visual art Conrad was conservative and far less well informed than many of his friends. Surely, however, it does not in any event follow that a literary impressionist would be instinctively attracted to impressionist painting; Conrad certainly was not. Yet his affinities with impressionist art lie deeper than oil paint and canvas in an epistemology that he recognized as both modern and revolutionary. In the awareness that there is no "realist" alternative to impressionism, that all complaisant norms are normal with a vengeance, Conrad had not jumped but dove head first into the twentieth century.

I raise the question of Ian Watt's creation of the phrase "delayed decoding"[3] partly so that I may stand on his shoulders (as I and so many others have often done before) and partly because the phrase leads naturally to his conclusion that "it is very unlikely that Conrad either thought of himself as an impressionist or was significantly influenced by the impressionist movement." Unlike so much of Watt's analysis in this book, that particular claim serves only to isolate Conrad from one of the most important aspects of early modernism. Readers of Conrad need not have read *Conrad in the Nineteenth Century* to surmise that by "delayed decoding" Watt means those moments—such as the attack on the steamer in *Heart of Darkness*—when the narrator sees and feels events without, at first, being able to name or explain them. Of all things Watt says about the process of these observations, the one quality he does not elicit seems to me the most important for connecting Conrad not only with impressionism but with epistemological currents at the turn of the century broader even than that movement.

In discussing "delayed decoding" in connection with Conrad's impressionism, we ought to recognize that the original undecoded observation ("Sticks, little sticks were flying about," to quote an appropriate example from *Heart of Darkness*) is terribly valuable to Conrad and not really undesirable temporary misunderstanding so much as an unmediated observation. In meticulously recording these uninterpreted or minimally interpreted observations—and they are often visual—Conrad reflects one of the original purposes of impressionism: to return to the most aboriginal sensation before concepts and rational categories are brought to bear. ("Arrows, by Jove! We were being shot at!")

There was an enduring Lockean impulse behind much early impressionist painting that required removing a good many of the mediating intellections in favor of the only irreducible sensation the painter had: the way it "seemed" to him. In painting, such a move often meant the deemphasis of drawing and perspective (both insistently intellectual abstractions, particularly as they appeared in French neoclassical painting) in favor of color and light and veils of atmosphere, the elimination of narrative elements in favor of the moment, and so on toward the accomplishment of unintellectualized immediacy, or at least the illusion of it. Parallel developments took place in philosophy, largely in Edmund

Bruce Johnson

Husserl's early work from roughly 1900 to 1913, in the *Logische Untersuchungen* and *Ideen I*.[4]

Husserl suggested that a "presuppositionless" philosophy had to trust the impression, not because it was in Locke's sense primary sensation which one could trust more than secondary ideas (and more than ideas based on ideas, the risk increasing toward the birth of "notions"), but because one could not challenge the simple claim that "this is the way it seemed to me." To the accusation that the individual had been mistaken, that "facts" later discovered or explanations later deduced had shown him to be wrong, the individual human consciousness might answer with Ford Madox Ford's narrator Dowell in *The Good Soldier,* "Isn't it true to say that for nine years I possessed a goodly apple?" For Husserl the subjective impression was the only trustworthy beginning for an ultimate grasp of essences. Although Husserl rather quickly moves toward an esoteric meditation on these impressions, his mood at the turn of the century, at the very moment *Lord Jim* was being published, is similar to Conrad's: to press back to the way it seemed ("but my feet felt so warm and wet that I had to look down") is to have puzzling access to truths largely obscured after the organizing concepts and causes and explanations have been imposed, after what is warm and wet becomes blood, death, attack, the natives' fear of losing Kurtz, and, finally, their fear of losing God—after little sticks become arrows and an absurdly treasured cane the shaft of a deadly spear. But to suggest that the intellections, the causes and categories and explanations, are somehow the "truth" encoded in the original sensation is to ignore an important aspect of the impressionist impulse and movement. The unexplained feeling of "warm and wet" is as true and valuable to Conrad as the concept "attack"—a concept, by the way, that the story subsequently shows to be genuinely imponderable. An examination of other instances

54

of Conrad's "delayed decoding" shows that the "explanations" are no more encoded in the original subjective sensation than a French neoclassical canvas would be in Monet's impressionist rendering of the scene.

Furthermore, when Watt says that "Conrad wanted to pay as much attention to the inside as to the outside, to the meaning as to the appearance" (p. 179), he is adopting a separation that to Husserl would have been discouragingly reminiscent of Kant's *noumenal* and *phenomenal* and to many impressionists would have ignored the meaning *in* the impression. There is a strong sense in which Husserl's long argument in *Logische Untersuchungen* is directed against just such a separation of meaning and appearance in those disciplines based upon an inadequate sense of how consciousness exists. Far more important than grasping Husserl's argument, however, must be the critic's sense that there is something in the *Zeitgeist* that produces both Husserl's and impressionism's defense of subjectivity against the increasingly strident claims of science to revealing in an orgy of "objectivity" the "inside" of Nature.

Thus, however much Conrad's impressionism may suggest relativity and even indeterminacy—no single view of Lord Jim having any real priority or authority over other equally coherent views—it also participates in the other crucial component of historic impressionism: a belief long-lived and probably stemming originally from the climate of Locke and Hume that the impression, the impress upon the mind of immediate sensual impulses, lies closer to the origin of meaning than the operation of subsequent thought. Clearly the relativism in impressionistic practice is prominent in Conrad's fiction, but the other historic component emerges at crucial moments and occasionally becomes a potent symbolic entrance to the most difficult meaning of the work. Although Conrad can, of course, no longer believe in anything like a

Lockean model of consciousness, he shares with that intellectual climate a passion for the origins of consciousness.

In a remarkable essay written in 1883 for a small exhibition of paintings by Pissarro, Degas, and Renoir, the poet Jules Laforgue emphasizes just the point I am making, that impressionism consists of returning the eye to, in his words, a "primitive" state where what the mind has learned can be stripped away from what the "natural eye" can truly apprehend: "a natural eye forgets tactile illusions and their convenient dead-language of line and acts only in its faculty of prismatic sensibility." "No line, light, relief, perspective, or chiaroscuro, none of those childish classifications."[5] Although the notion of primitive, original "impression" is no longer Lockean or derived immediately from Hume, the new Young-Helmholtz theory of color vision and the famous Weber's or Fechner's law for measuring the intensity of sensation allow a nineteenth-century scientific version of the same basic metaphor for the mind. The impressionists invariably believe, as Jules Laforgue does, that their painting has returned to what the eye intrinsically does in its natural or primitive state, before it has been reshaped by what the tactile senses know and what all kinds of intervening intellection may demand as the proper emphasis of painting. Such demands may even call for an historical motif as the structuring aesthetic principle (not, say, a patch of coastal water in the sunlight but the death of Socrates or the oath of the Horatii). In short, all the new scientific and quasi-scientific theories of color and vision that inform impressionism only serve to confirm the impressionist's intuition that he has reached back to some kind of original seeing, and that such perception offers a kind of truth quickly eroded with the impositions of reason and the special perceptions of other senses, particularly of the tactile sense.

There seems little reason to believe that Conrad's "delayed

decoding" departs in any important way from this general impressionist practice. Of course not all of Conrad's main instances of "delayed decoding" depend quite so much on the eye as those in *Heart of Darkness*. But virtually all of them imply not so much an initial misunderstanding that will subsequently "clear up" as they do an initial unguarded perception whose meaning may be far more revealing to the reader than the subsequent "decoding." The fact that arrows seem at first to be "little sticks" may reveal more about the ambiguous attitude of Kurtz's natives toward these intruders, and about Kurtz's functioning among them as a god, than the subsequently official and rather self-limiting definition of this very complex set of events and feelings as, simply, an "attack." One of the main points of the journey upriver is that increasingly almost nothing can confidently be "read"; traditional meanings and traditional names no longer function, and along with the "pilgrim" who is no real pilgrim we cry out, "'Good God! What is the meaning—?'"

In such an atmosphere there can be no secure decoding— largely because there has been no sense of meaning encoded. The metaphor of coding and decoding erodes. As Marlow soon notes, there was more "desperate" grief than threat in "the savage clamour that had swept by us on the river-bank." Of the arrows themselves, neither Marlow nor the reader knows whether they are poisoned or, as they seem, "wouldn't kill a cat." Francis Ford Coppola in *Apocalypse Now* obviously thinks the arrows are *essentially* "little sticks" because he has his Marlow-assassin call out something like "Can't you see they're just trying to frighten us? Those arrows won't hurt you." All the familiarity that Conrad employs in describing the death of the helmsman, the *impression* of the helmsman's death, constitutes not a misunderstanding that must subsequently be straightened out with identifications such as "spear," "blood," and "death" in place of "a long cane," something "warm and wet," and the intimate gesture of the helmsman clutching "that cane." On the contrary, the "impression" apparently contained for Conrad a truth not available once the intellect and its categories of cause and effect had begun to work in Marlow: that violent death instantly becomes a paradoxically intimate experience, in which the very instrument of death may well seem a personal possession, "like something precious," the victim "afraid I would try to take it away from him." We are not invited to suppose that in this last impressionistic supposition Marlow has been wildly wrong, that no victim would regard the instrument of his certain death as a precious personal possession. Most assuredly the text is haunted by the possibility that the rapidly dying helmsman (suddenly confronted by the most irrevocably personal event of his life) might paradoxically feel just this way. Even the apparent temporary validity of the explanation that this is largely a violent attack is finally undercut when the "angry and war-like yells" stop instantly and are replaced by a "tremulous and prolonged wail of mournful fear and utter despair." If we cannot tell whether this is an attack in any ordinary sense of the word—despair more than anger, an act of worship perhaps more than anything—the apparently misguided first impressions become peculiarly authoritative.

In order to confirm my sense that Conrad's use of this device is not only impressionistic in a way that owes a good deal to the larger aesthetic movement but also peculiarly revealing of the novel's guiding epistemology, we need to move on to a later instance in *The Secret Agent*. Throughout this novel we recognize that the border between organic and inorganic is continually blurred and violated. The street that Mr. Verloc enters on his way to the embassy "in its breadth, emptiness, and extent . . . had the majesty of inorganic nature, of matter that never dies." "And the thick police constable, looking a stranger to every emotion, as if he, too, were part of inorganic nature, surging apparently out of a lamp-post took not the slightest notice of Mr. Verloc." This is the novel, after all, in which Mrs. Verloc imagines that "after a rainlike fall of mangled limbs the decapitated head of Stevie lingered suspended above, and fading out slowly like the last star of a pyrotechnic display." Certainly it is by no means clear that this ontological blurring is always impressionistic in the sense of the "primitive" or "natural eye" mentioned by Laforgue, but many readers have felt that it is indeed the peculiar "Lebenswelt" of this novel.

In the scene I should like to discuss, Winnie has just stabbed Verloc in what paradoxically might appear to be merely a decorous extension of their "respectable home life." "To the last its decorum had remained undisturbed by unseemly shrieks and other misplaced sincerities of conduct." As Winnie leans over the couch on which Verloc, quietly dead, reclines, she looks "at the clock with inquiring mistrust. She had become aware of a ticking sound in the room." The reader has no way of knowing, almost until Winnie does, that the ticking sound is no mechanical measure of abstract time but the dripping of Verloc's blood. As the interval between drops or "ticks" diminishes, and the sound approaches that of a continual flow of life's blood, "as if the trickle had been the first sign of a destroying flood," we recognize that all the symbolic suggestiveness of the attack on Greenwich mean time here intersects with the ontological blurring of the inanimate and animate, abstract time with the time measured by drops of human blood, time and human life finally measured in the same medium; and this intersection is all permeated with the flood allusion, the cleansing flood that brings no new covenant and on the contrary a "free" Winnie. It is appropriate that having fully identified the sound, she flees the room by giving the table a push "as though it had been alive." Verloc's round hat, which had earlier sought the cover of the table like some fugitive cat or dog, becomes a hat again when the table is moved and rocks "slightly on its crown in the wind of her flight."

In short, the original illusion, that the dripping blood had been the even ticking of the clock, provides not a random misunderstanding that is subsequently cleared up but a stunning preparation for all the symbolic complication available when we connect with the murder of Verloc the role that abstract, measured time has played in this novel with the murder of Verloc. Somehow the relationship of these rational, order-giving abstractions (Greenwich standard time) with anarchy and with the passions that actually create the illusions of ideal order have not crystalized until Winnie's confusion of the ticking clock with the dripping blood; it is less a confusion than a fusion, a fusion of the inanimate and animate that has haunted the text from the beginning. A good case can be made for saying that the crisis of the novel lies not in Stevie's demolition or even in the moment of the stabbing but only in these imagistic reflections by Winnie on both murders.

It strikes me that a good part of Conrad's "delayed decoding" resembles the attempt of Hemingway and before him of Mark Twain to recognize that there is no such thing as an isolated and meaningful fact or event or object. Meaning, as William Barrett argues in his book *Time of Need* while discussing Hemingway and other moderns, is a function of connectedness.[6] The meaning we see in an apparently discreet moment or event depends on the conceptual and emotional "net" we use to capture it. (This metaphor is Iris Murdoch's in her first novel called *Under the Net* and probably derives from her reading in phenomenology and her experience of Wittgenstein at Oxford.) Tom Sawyer's literary expectations and the Grangerfords' code of the blood feud

are two such compelling systems of meaning that they begin
to affect what one can see in the first place. We may recognize
in the kind of critical analysis appropriate to these writers a
congruence of Gestalt psychology with early phenomenology,
both of them products of the period from roughly 1900 to
1913 or '14, although in American literature and in William
James and Charles Peirce we find many anticipations of such
epistemological analysis.[7] Melville himself develops a similar
technique for *Moby Dick* and there are clearly enough reasons in the special plight of mid-nineteenth-century American consciousness to explain why this technique of "I look,
we look, ye look" may have been an American talent even
before it became Husserl's. The influence from William
James to Husserl is slowly and recently becoming clear, were
one to pursue this rather elegant transatlantic connection. In
any event, Stephen Crane was himself immersed in the
awareness; one can see it emerging from the wooden naturalism of *Maggie: A Girl of the Streets* and, despite Conrad's
private undervaluing of Crane's impressionism in *The Red
Badge of Courage,* watch its flowering in that novel.

The point is that having understood how preconceived
"nets" of meaning instantly trap an event, sight, sound, comment, alleged "fact" or what have you, the fledgling phenomenologist begins to relish two basic maneuvers. First, to
reveal how what seemed to be a random impression (say, the
apparent ticking of a clock) was in truth instantly ensnared in
a matrix of connectedness, could not perhaps have even been
perceived had not an appropriate net been already present
and active. Can we even *perceive* what is essentially uncon-
nected or meaningless? Clocks and time are, after all, a very
important preoccupation for Conrad in this novel, for the
reader of *The Secret Agent,* and for Winnie, who in caring
"nothing for time" indicates the author's deep involvement
with it. Another author or character might instantly have

attributed another meaning to the measured sound, as any Gestalt psychologist would argue.

The second fascination for the beginning phenomenologist lies in the possibility that there may be a kind of pristine though not necessarily innocent perceiving outside the nets, that one may cultivate a certain talent for lifting them; *aletheia*, which William Barrett translates as "unhiddenness," may be a different sort of truth from that suggested by the German *wahr*, connected with "*bewahren*, to guard or preserve."[8] While not actually participating in Husserl's cry of "Zu den Sachen selbst!" an important vein of literary impressionism, certainly in part Conrad and Crane, participates in this phenomenological urgency that is so broadly characteristic of the turn of the century. (Husserl's search for a "presuppositionless" philosophy begins, I repeat, with *Logische Untersuchungen* in 1900 and runs in its pure early form to *Ideen I* in 1913.)

Conrad is anxious to recreate those rather rare moments when we perceive something that is either genuinely outside the usual nets and must subsequently be contained (as a sudden, surprising occurrence may be) or, more likely, when we perceive something that only appears to be pristine in this way. In brief, it is vital to Conrad's moral sense that he reveal again and again the value of this phenomenological perceiving (on those rare occasions when it may be possible) and — the more likely occasion — that he show his readers how perception usually depends on the preconceptions, the emotional and intellectual Gestalten that make the perception possible in the first place. Thus "delayed decoding" is an important part of both Conrad's and Crane's larger experiments with these preconceptions, of their attempts to reveal how perception depends on Gestalten that may be as manic and overt as the Swede's regarding the Wild West in Crane's "The Blue Hotel" or as subtly pervasive and controlling as

Henry Fleming's sense of war as heroic struggle and epic denouement (even though positively "Greeklike struggle," Henry imagines, was probably a thing of the past). Henry retains enough of this preconception to be singularly disappointed that in seeing him off to war his mother says "nothing whatever about returning with his shield or on it." As *The Red Badge of Courage* develops, Henry's controlling assumptions wax and wane; new variations of the "epic struggle" mind-set emerge and are immediately challenged by events that Henry is usually not prepared to receive. Most especially, the central issue in his mind, whether he shall be courageous or a coward, is in its very dichotomous stiffness a function of his epic mind-set. We need not go on to show that in this kind of analysis *The Red Badge* is a virtuoso performance that had begun with the perceptions of Maggie in *Maggie: A Girl of the Streets* and, interestingly enough, may have entered the mainstream of literary impressionism from the crisis to which Crane brought naturalistic assumptions in that novel. As a would-be naturalist in *Maggie*, Crane had seen that if environment determines character (as the colon in the novel's title insists), environment is a perceived thing: to Maggie, Pete is "a knight," to cite only one extreme instance of this truth.

Conrad gives Lord Jim a mind-set that he may very well have learned from watching Crane's performance in *The Red Badge,* though to reviewers who pointed out similarities and suggested an influence on *The Nigger of the "Narcissus,"* Conrad answered that he had not read *The Red Badge* until after *The Nigger* had been finished. As I said in an article many years ago, his sensitivity to the alleged influence from the younger master may have led him to experiment with his own memory, even though he admired Crane and his work.[9] Although in letters Conrad disparaged Crane's "impressionism" as largely a taste for striking metaphors, Conrad's own

Lord Jim begins his career so full of the assumptions, so equipped with the screens and blinders of "light" adventure stories that his conception of heroism and heroic honor will never change. These "thoughts . . . full of valorous deeds" were "the best parts of life, its secret truth, its hidden reality." The crew of the *Patna* did not matter; "Those men did not belong to the world of heroic adventure." His measure of life is "a hero in a book." It is my sense—though critics have always disagreed on the issue—that this screen of heroic adventure, this special set of colored glasses, continues right through the end of the novel, determining how Jim imagines he can use Patusan, Jewel, Brown, and determining to the end his conception of both heroism and redemption. In a world where most people seek their experience through the medium of such Gestalten, moments of phenomenological "unhiddenness," *aletheia,* become especially precious to the author, though the author may well make his character regard them as mistakes, or as confusion later to be decoded with conventional or traditional categories and explanations. Many of these perceptions will subsequently (in the course of the text) be shown to have been no unhiddenness at all but to have been generated by preconceptions so subtle and so much a part of the culture that neither character nor reader or even author could initially have detected the net. William Bonney has shown how Conrad works endlessly with the rubrics of traditional romance in this regard, and how the expectations of readers steeped in such Western romance epistemology are deliberately aroused and then undercut.[10]

No doubt both Conrad and Crane were skeptical about the possibility that any such true "unhiddenness" existed. Yet many passages in their work testify to a curiosity about such possibilities. When Henry Fleming has run from the battle, his mind frantically experiments with variations of an anthropomorphized Nature, of an intention in Nature. He trips and stumbles, and so Nature, he momentarily feels, is inimical to his flight. When, moments later in relative quiet, he throws a pine cone at a squirrel and watches it flee, Nature, he concludes, is teaching him one of its laws: that it is only natural to flee danger. Finally, still exploring the feeling that he may only have acted naturally and that this now-benevolent Nature has conducted him to a "chapel" of trees in the forest in order that he find a measure of peace in its bosom, he discovers in the "chapel" near where the altar would have been, a "thing," the corpse of a soldier with ants "trundling some sort of a bundle along the upper lip" and "venturing horribly near to the eyes." In the midst of anthropomorphic preconceptions and emotional presuppositions that turn almost anything into intentions and tall trees into a chapel, he finds this moment of *aletheia,* the unhidden revelation that Nature is indifferent process. The eyes may be window to the soul, but not to ants about their natural business.

Crane's rhetoric is as busy in the image of the ants as it had been in the other details of Henry's flight from battle, and of course Henry's "red badge of courage" might also be recognized as a red badge of cowardice if the circumstances of his head wound were known. Yet Crane's intention in the title is not simply ironic but to play, rather, upon the epistemological implications of the word *badge.* Nothing is a badge absolutely. Only relative to a particular mind-set, to a presupposed web of connectedness, can something signify in the manner suggested by the word *badge.* Thus questions that critics have vigorously debated about whether Crane intends us to feel that Henry has in some sense "redeemed" his earlier flight or has been both coward and hero in so short a time are all subsumed in these larger epistemological interests. Concerned as he may be to push his absurdest view of man's place in the cosmos (epitomized by the waving tourists on the beach in the "The Open Boat," a story that Conrad found "fundamentally interesting"), Crane is far more interested in problems of perception and signification that are central to historic impressionism.

My pleasure in Conrad's approach to these issues comes both from impressions such as those during the "attack" in *Heart of Darkness* and from such moments as the dripping blood mistaken for the ticking clock in *The Secret Agent*. Whether the "unhiddenness" is only illusory, with, in fact, potent presuppositions already at work selecting and filtering, as they are in Winnie's mind, or the perception is genuinely phenomenological, Conrad seems willing to suspend the kind of barely sublimated rhetoric that we often find at similar moments in Stephen Crane. He is so much a student of what the world might be were it perceived even for a moment outside these nets that he willingly suspends rhetoric that might have tempted him. Carried to a kind of reductio ad absurdum, a similar technique characterizes, in theory at least, the novels of Alain Robbe-Grillet or the inexplicably lingering camera work in *Last Year at Marienbad*. In Conrad, such experiments reveal their turn-of-the-century tentativeness, but they nonetheless participate in a phenomenological sensitivity densely entangled by the first few years of the century with the practice and theory of impressionism.

The principal strategy of Husserl's work from 1900 to just before the war is to suggest that subjective impression, far from being the antagonist of scientific, objective observation, is the *only* unimpeachable perception and provides the high road to true essences. To a cultural historian in the 1980s, Husserl's use of the impression may seem a peculiarly odd and Germanic defense of the value of subjectivity. But impressionism had already schooled itself (as Laforgue's essay suggests) in the proper methods for divesting one's perception of presuppositions arising from senses other than sight,

66

"tactile illusions and their convenient dead language of line," to cite only one example.

Impressionism's passion to return to the "primitive eye" is no doubt involved in the larger taste of all early modernism for analysis in terms of origins, in *The Waste Land* no less than in Frazer, Freud, and Marx. When all kinds of orthodox foundations have crumbled, the suspicion has usually been that they were not fundamental enough to stand, that one had not gone down to bedrock. Since the entire impetus of *Heart of Darkness* is toward such origins, in morality ("restraint"), language, and consciousness itself, it would be very unusual indeed if these instances of unrehearsed perception were not at some level in Conrad's mind analogous to his destination upriver, to the "primitive" form of things, which turns out not to be necessarily savage at all. As in most elements of this story the putatively "civilized" becomes the most genuinely savage, so "civilized" perception, where items are duly registered in nets of traditional or customary signification at once, can readily become a form of violence. Marlow begins to see in this pristine way only when the steamer has very symbolically entered fog and seems about to lose all moorings, all sense of direction; Marlow himself by this time has come to suspect the conventional moorings of "civilization" (particularly as to language) in precisely the sense that he has seen these nets used with the utmost violence to define the "enemies" of "progress" and of "civilization." He is prepared for the risk of seeing in this naïve way.

Claude Monet is reported to have said:

When you go out to paint, try to forget what objects you have before you—a tree, a house, a field, or whatever. Merely think, here is a little square of blue, here an oblong of pink, here a streak of yellow, and paint it just as it looks to you, the exact color and shape, until it gives your own naïve impression of the scene before you.

He said he wished he had been born blind and then had suddenly gained his sight so that he could have begun to paint in this way without knowing what the objects were that he saw before him.[11]

In this revolutionary comment we of course recognize a continuation of the modernist impulse to purge art of extraneous rhetoric and to move toward "pure" art; but the comment also implies a phenomenological flavor not unlike Husserl's "bracketing," the famous *epoché* necessary to wrest a thing from the nets of tradition, convention, and even existence. As would Husserl, Conrad approaches the so-called "attack" with an openness and a respect for the truly apodictic (the compellingly *present* to the viewer) that does not initially seek explanations or theories but follows the spirit of Wittgenstein's admonition: "Describe, don't explain." The few comparisons (the helmsman holding the "cane" as though someone might try to take it from him) are not offered primarily as explanations or theories about what has happened but as the sort of imaginative flexibility with the immediate experience that Husserl recommended in order to intensify the looking. The true spirit of *epoché* refused to establish quickly and prejudicially hierarchies of what might be very real, less real, or not so real about the experience.[12] The *epoché* is to be found elsewhere in impressionism and early modernism, and represents a generosity about subjective experience, a refusal to constrict it with preconceived theories about what is "real" or even about the nature of subjectivity itself. The associations Marlow makes with the puzzling events before his eyes serve only to open him to the experience, to make him see more intently and with fewer prejudgments than he or the reader can usually manage. We do not await the "true" explanation of all these strange actions so much as we recognize subsequently the value of such looking, such perception, when confronted with the spectacle of Marlow's experience of Kurtz. Clearly Conrad feels we must be prepared for this kind of perceiving before we arrive at our destination. Like the Accountant, the Lawyer, and the Director of Companies, we are too well equipped with ready-made judgments that immediately constrict our ability to perceive. Husserl does not pull the idea of *epochē* out of thin air but out of the rich context of an increasingly positivist nineteenth century. Of course the maneuver is in Monet made in the name of optical integrity, but had it been made in the name of an equivalent integrity for all the senses and for the act of perception in general the effect and the spirit would be very similar to Conrad.

In this peculiar and virtually unnoticed coincidence of impressionism and phenomenology at the turn of the century, a cultural historian has a unique opportunity for uncovering an aspect of early modernism that probably has not yet been given a name. If Kurtz and Marlow have not also "been born blind" and then suddenly gained their sight, they are assuredly among those early moderns who have found it necessary to work toward the primordial origins of consciousness, in the manner of those other pioneers (surely John Locke among them) who feel required to do so at the beginning of any new "period" in human consciousness.

When the little sticks begin flying two hours after the "cotton-wool" fog has lifted (that time when to let go the bottom would have meant being "absolutely in the air—in space"), Conrad offers us not confused seeing, but a "freshness of sensory perception" that William Barrett in describing Hemingway's story "Big Two-Hearted River" has called the "morning of the world."[13] The whole episode of the fog and the "attack" is introduced by Marlow's puzzlement at the cannibal crew's "restraint"—his astonishment that in their hunger they do not simply eat the "pilgrims." ("Restraint! What possible restraint? Was it superstition, disgust, patience, fear—or some kind of primitive honour?") This restraint is to him a "greater mystery" than the "inexplicable note of desperate grief in this savage clamour that had swept by us on the river-bank behind the blind whiteness of the fog." The reader's mind is invited to substitute one "mystery" for another and finally to regard even the "attack" (the pilgrims' word) as all but imponderable in abstract terms: "What we afterwards alluded to as an attack was really an attempt at repulse. The action was very far from being aggressive—it was not even defensive, in the usual sense: it was undertaken under the stress of desperation, and in its essence was purely protective."

The only things we can rely on in this devolution of abstract, traditional language and categories are the utterly fresh, sensory perceptions, now somehow freed from the conventional expectations that might have persisted in Conrad's audience, had not all of us by now gone so far upriver toward, to use Conrad's phrase, "the beginnings of time." And of course what we are ultimately left with is the utterly fresh sensuous impression of Kurtz, largely as a voice, beyond any of the abstractions that might have kept this presence from us or have screened it in conventional ways. It has, in short, been necessary to create the morning of the world because, whether he is corrupt or heroic or both, that is where this character stands. We can now begin to create afresh whatever abstractions we may design to contain Kurtz, but always with the sure sense that we have experienced for a moment the world all but emptied of them.

Hunt Hawkins

Conrad and the Psychology of Colonialism

Most of the fiction from the first five years of Conrad's writing career (from 1895 to 1900) was based on his personal observation as a sailor during the previous two decades. The principal locations for these stories are the colonies of the Malay Archipelago and the Congo. Initially hailed simply as romantic tales because of their exotic settings, Conrad's stories may now be appreciated as profound studies, nearly unique in English literature, of the colonial situation. The stories speak of many other topics, of course, but Conrad was keenly interested in the dynamics of colonialism, especially its psychology. In his early fiction he explored a particular type of colonial locale, the trading outpost, and examined the peculiar transformations brought about in both the European colonialists and the colonized natives through their encounter.

In describing the psychology of colonialism, Conrad relied to a certain extent on the concepts of contemporary philosophers and sociologists, notably Herbert Spencer, St. George Mivart, and Edward von Hartmann.[1] But Conrad is remarkable for the degree to which he went beyond the thinking of his period. His portrayal of the colonial situation is quite complex and is, in many ways, a brilliant forerunner of the most noted modern study of the subject, O. Mannoni's *Prospero and Caliban: The Psychology of Colonization,* published in 1950. Mannoni, a French ethnographer who lived in Madagascar, developed reciprocal theories explaining the colonialists and the colonized. For his analysis of the European, Mannoni used a combination of Adlerian psychoanalytic theory and phenomenology. The following description summarizes his analysis:

> What the colonial in common with Prospero lacks is awareness of the world of Others—a world in which others have to be respected. This is the world from which the colonial has fled because he cannot accept men as they are. Rejection of the world is combined with an urge to dominate, an urge which is infantile in origin, and which social adaptation has failed to discipline. The reason the colonial himself gives for his flight—whether he says it was the desire to travel, or the desire to escape from the cradle or from the "ancient parapets," or whether he says that he simply wanted a freer life—is of no consequence, for whatever the variant offered, the real reason is still what I have called loosely the colonial vocation. It is always a question of compromising with the desire for a world without men.[2]

The colonialists, of course, have economic motives for going to Asia or Africa, but such motives are fully complementary with more intangible psychological ones. According to Mannoni, the typical colonialist, unable to succeed in European society, becomes the victim of an inferiority complex. He flees to the colonial situation where, through no real merit of his own, he is put in a position of dominance. The colonialist does not and cannot enter into community with the natives because they lack freedom and are unable to interact with him as equals; they remain objects upon which he projects his own schemes and fantasies. The isolation of the colonialist in his superior position, while gratifying certain compelling needs, ultimately leads to psychological instability and disintegration. Conrad expressed his own perception of this paradoxical colonial fate in the story "Youth" (1898) when Marlow says, "I have seen the mysterious shores, the still water, the lands of brown nations, where a stealthy Nemesis lies in wait, pursues, overtakes so many of the conquering race."[3]

An examination of Conrad's fiction shows that all of his main colonial figures live in a "world without men." In his first two novels, *Almayer's Folly* (1895) and *An Outcast of the Islands* (1896), both set in the Malay Archipelago, the primary psychological category used is that of *will*. The two central figures, Kaspar Almayer and Peter Willems, are men who suffer a failure of will and become immobilized. We can see that their loss of will is connected with the fact that they have denied the will of the others around them. As Mannoni notes: "If a man lives in the midst of his own projections without truly admitting the independent will and existence of other people, he loses his own will and his own independence, while the *ego* inflates as it becomes empty" (p. 114).

Kaspar Almayer is a man who has had a weak will from the outset. We should note that he was born in Java and has never been to Europe. Thus he has never existed outside a colonial situation. He has married a native woman and moved to Sambir not through his own initiative but at the behest of his mentor, Tom Lingard. He stays in Sambir for twenty-five years, unable to leave even though his trade has failed. He dreams of becoming wealthy, then going to a Europe he can only imagine. All his hope rests in Lingard's nebulous "mountain of gold." After Lingard disappears, Almayer finds another person to wait around for—his supposed assistant, Dain Maroola. Toward the end, Almayer's immobilization takes on increasingly conclusive forms: his face becomes stonelike, he begins smoking opium, and finally he dies.

Almayer is a racist, and all of his relations with other people are relations with objects. He says to the visiting Dutch officers: "It is a great pleasure to see white faces here. I have lived here many years in solitude. The Malays, you understand, are not company for white men; moreover they are not friendly; they do not understand our ways" (*Almayer's Folly,* p. 122). Almayer sees his wife merely as a tool to get Lingard's money. He believes that it will be "easy enough to dispose of a Malay woman, a slave after all" (pp. 10–11). Later on, although he is not able to "dispose" of her, their relationship deteriorates and she leaves the house. Even Lingard is not seen as an equal. He is "Father," all-powerful, munificent, unpredictable.

Almayer's most curious relationship is with his own daughter, Nina. In *An Outcast of the Islands,* a novel set some twenty years earlier, Almayer is described as worshipping the child Nina as a "small god" (p. 122). Nina is the principal object of Almayer's fantasies. He envisages her parading through Europe: "Nobody would think of her mixed blood in the presence of her great beauty and of his immense wealth. Witnessing her triumphs he would grow young again" (*Almayer's Folly,* pp. 3–4). In effect, what Almayer does is to transfer the responsibility for his actions to his daughter. He believes he has done everything for her. By making her the central cause, he betrays his own independent will.

Nina herself recognizes the inhuman aspect of their relation. In running off with Dain Maroola, she says she wants love, not gold; life, not thinghood. She believes that with Dain neither of them is an object; both are subjects. Here she describes her relationship with Dain to Almayer: "You were speaking of gold then, but our ears were filled with the song of our love, and we did not hear you. Then I found that we could see through each other's eyes: that he saw things that nobody but myself and he could see. We entered a land where no one could follow us, and least of all you. Then I began to live" (*Almayer's Folly,* p. 179). Nina has other motives, of course, among them to use Dain Maroola as an instrument for revenge against the whites who rejected her, but her criticism of Almayer is accurate.

Peter Willems is in many ways similar to Almayer. Like Almayer, he marries a native woman (Joanna is so defined because she is a half-caste) in order to improve his financial prospects by pleasing an authority figure, her secret father, the Dutch Trader Hudig. Willems also resembles Almayer in that he lets Lingard dump him in Sambir.

Willems's feelings of inferiority and the compensations he gets from the colonial situation are made clear enough by his relationship with his wife's dark-skinned relatives, the Da Souzas: "That family's admiration was the great luxury of his life. It rounded and completed his existence in a perpetual assurance of unquestionable superiority. He loved to breathe the coarse incense they offered before the shrine of the successful white man" (*Outcast,* pp. 3–4).

Willems's most interesting relationship is with Omar's daughter, Aissa. Mannoni says of a European man who falls in love with a native woman: "Psychologically he is one with Pygmalion; he can only love his own creation, his own *anima*" (p. 111). Since the woman is his own projection, she has no will in relation to him and his own will collapses. Willems's love for Aissa is described in just these terms. He sees himself as "the slave of a passion he had always derided, as the man unable to assert his will" (*Outcast,* p. 128). We know Willems cares little for Aissa as a person independent of his own fantasies because he falls in love before having spoken with her, he has no sympathy for her wearing a veil in the presence of Abdulla, and in the end his "love" disappears completely. Willems views Aissa merely as a thing. Despite his claim that he has "no colour prejudices and no racial antipathies" (p. 35), he sees his "love" as "surrendering to a wild creature the unstained purity of his life, of his race, of his civilization" (p. 80).

In one telling instance, after the love has gone, Willems reacts to Aissa's staring at him. Her gaze, like Sartre's "look," transforms her into the subject and him into the object. Willems cannot stand this. As a white, he is supposed to be the subject. He says, "Look at her eyes. Ain't they big? Don't they stare? . . . They follow me like a pair of jailers. . . . They are big, menacing—and empty. The eyes of a savage; of a damned mongrel, half-Arab, half-Malay. They hurt me! I am white! I swear to you I can't stand this! Take me away. I am white! All white!" (*Outcast*, pp. 270–71).

Willems, of course, does not sink into quite the same stupefied immobility as Almayer. Rather he lets himself be used by Babalatchi and Abdulla as a tool against Lingard. Lingard then isolates him with Aissa, who kills him.

At first sight Tom Lingard is a much more attractive figure than either Almayer or Willems. He is a "man of purpose" rather than an immobilized will. He is active, successful, and benevolent. Even Babalatchi says to him, "Amongst the whites, who are devils, you are a man" (*Outcast*, p. 227).

But on closer examination Lingard also appears to be living in the colonialist "world without men." The source of Lingard's motivation in feelings of inferiority is clearly brought out in the third novel of the trilogy, *The Rescue* (begun 1896, published 1920). Lingard, an ex–trawler boy from Devonshire, tells the upperclass Englishman Mr. Travers, "If I hadn't been an adventurer, I would have had to starve or work at home for such people as you" (*Rescue*, p. 134). In the archipelago, Lingard becomes a king, Rajah Laut, but he is not committed to Malayan society. Rather, he dreams of going back to Devonshire as a rich man. Like

Almayer, he has an unrealistic fantasy about his "mountain of gold" and what it can bring. Like Willems, he has trouble believing in his own success as a trader. In the end Lingard wrecks his brig, the *Flash*, loses his monopoly of the Pantai, and goes broke.

The primary way Lingard turns others into objects is through a peculiar sort of paternalism. Both Almayer and Mrs. Almayer call him "Father." But, as Almayer points out, Lingard's benevolence toward people usually ends in disaster. Lingard killed Mrs. Almayer's father and then adopted her. He sent her to a convent school in Samarang and then married her to Almayer. After the birth of Nina, he capriciously shifted all his affection to the child and, as far as we can tell, never gave another thought to Mrs. Almayer. And we have already seen the result of Lingard's benevolence toward Almayer and Williams.

Lingard plans "Arcadian happiness" for the natives on the Pantai, "his" river. But Conrad notes, "His deep-seated and immovable conviction that only he—he, Lingard—knew what was good for them was characteristic of him. . . . He would make them happy whether or no, he said, and he meant it" (*Outcast*, p. 200). It does not really matter that for a while Lingard brought peace and prosperity to Sambir. As far as Lingard was concerned, the natives were not free and their wishes were of no consequence. They were only objects to be manipulated to satisfy his own ego and his simple European conception of benevolence.

The hero of *Lord Jim* (1900) is another character who at first sight appears attractive, one who has avoided the isolating arrogance of the colonialist. Jim is committed to living in Patusan and is shown helping the natives rather than exploiting them (even though he does maintain a profitable trading post for Stein). Finally, he appears to submit himself to native justice by letting Doramin shoot him.

On closer examination, however, we find that Jim, too, is

living in a "world without men," that the natives are for him mere objects in his own project. Jim's driving motive is to recover the romantic idea of himself which he lost when he deserted the *Patna*. He wants to prove to himself that he has courage and is trustworthy. Since his past continually haunts him, Jim cannot accomplish these goals in the world of European men. He cannot escape his feelings of inferiority. Therefore he is driven to a remote corner of Borneo, to Patusan, to the natives, and to the colonial situation.

Jim makes a success of himself in Patusan. After he escapes from Rajah Allang's stockade, and later after he defeats Sherif Ali, he virtually rules the community. The natives regard him as having "supernatural powers." But how does Jim regard them? They are counters he needs to bolster his self-image through their trust in him. Jim consequently becomes dependent upon them and cannot leave the colonial situation. He is stuck in Patusan just as Almayer and Willems are stuck in Sambir. Jim says, "I must feel—every day, every time I open my eyes—that I am trusted—that nobody has a right—don't you know? Leave? For where? What for? To get what?" (p. 247). And in another place he says to Marlow, "I must stick to their belief in me to feel safe and to—to . . . to keep in touch with . . . with those whom, perhaps, I shall never see any more. With—with—you, for instance" (p. 334).

At one point Marlow claims that Jim has managed to detach himself from the European perspective. He says that Jim "had no dealings but with himself and the question is whether at the last he had not confessed to a faith mightier than the laws of order and progress" (p. 339). Marlow is right in that Jim had no allegiance to the imperial "civilizing mission," but it is not true that Jim broke free from the European world. All his actions are taken not in reference to Patusan, but to a European idea of honor. He is constantly imagining what Europeans would think of him. Unfortunately, Jim is never fully able to redeem his sense of his own trustworthiness because he does not regard the trust of the natives, upon which he is so dependent, as equivalent to European trust. After two years in Patusan, he still feels that Marlow would not want him as a hand on his ship. And in this last interview with the older man, Jim says, "The very thought of the world outside is enough to give me a fright" (p. 305).

The final proof of Jim's continued sense of inferiority and his attachment to Europe comes when he releases the misanthropic criminal Gentleman Brown and thereby betrays his ties with the natives, who oppose his action. Brown plays upon Jim's feelings of kinship. They are similar people in being outcast from European society and in their fear of European judgment. Probably the appeal that affects Jim most, by recalling the *Patna* episode, is Brown's statement about his surrounded crew: "There are my men in the same boat—and, by God, I am not the sort to jump out of trouble and leave them in a d——d lurch" (pp. 382–83). Jim feels empathy for Brown and makes the disastrous decision to let him go. Gentleman Brown repays the kindness by gratuitously killing Dain Waris and his men.

During their negotiations Jim deals with Brown as a fellow human being and senses that Brown sees into him. On the other hand, Jim believes the natives cannot really know him: "They can't be made to understand what is going on in me" (p. 306). For Jim, the natives are always objects, never subjects. In Patusan, as Marlow says, Jim exists in a state of "total and utter isolation" (p. 272). He is "alone of his own superior kind" (p. 176).

What is the meaning of Jim's last act? Many readers have seen his submission of his life to Doramin as a positive gesture, one in which he regains his honor and affirms his allegiance to the native community. In the present perspective, however, Jim continues to live in a "world without men." Conrad's language indicates that Jim is acting on a self-centered notion of honor when he leaves Jewel to go to Doramin: "We can see him . . . tearing himself out of the arms of a jealous love at the sign, at the call of his exalted egoism. He goes away from a living woman to celebrate his pitiless wedding with a shadowy ideal of conduct" (p. 416).

Jim never seems to abandon his egoism for the world of others. His "love" for Jewel (a figure similar to Willems's Aissa) is merely a relation with an object who trusts him. In the end he leaves her for a stronger proof of his honor—namely, his own death.

The most spectacular example of isolation among Conrad's colonialists—and indeed among all the figures of modern literature—is Kurtz in *Heart of Darkness* (1899). The origin of Kurtz's colonial career in feelings of inferiority might not be readily apparent, since he is described as a supremely talented individual. He is a journalist, a painter, and an electrifying speaker who could have gone into politics. Towards the end of the novel we learn that he was also a "great musician" who had "the making of an immense success" (p. 153). But Kurtz was thwarted in European society. When Marlow interviews the Intended, he finds that "her engagement with Kurtz had been disapproved by her people. He wasn't rich enough or something. And indeed I don't know whether he had not been a pauper all his life. He had given me some reason to infer that it was his impatience of comparative poverty that drove him out there" (p. 159).

Kurtz's chief initial motive in going to the Congo seems to have been the desire to make money and rise in the European social scale. Once in Africa, Kurtz discovers other gratifications in the colonial situation, but even at the very end of his life he is still dreaming of returning to Europe and having "kings meet him at railway stations" (p. 148). In her book

The Origins of Totalitarianism, Hannah Arendt seems correct in seeing Kurtz as a representative of the "superfluous men" who are "an inevitable residue of the capitalist system." She compares Kurtz, with his European-bred sense of inferiority, to the German explorer Carl Peters, who went to Africa saying he "was fed up with being counted among the pariahs and wanted to belong to a master race."[4]

Many readers, including F. R. Leavis, have complained that Kurtz's crimes in the Congo are not stated definitely enough. We know that he took a native mistress, armed a lake tribe to raid the rest of the country for ivory, and put the heads of "rebels" on posts around his hut. The supposed indefiniteness comes when we are told that Kurtz presided "at certain midnight dances ending with unspeakable rites" (p. 118). Quite probably these rites were human sacrifices. In any case, Conrad does tell us explicitly what Kurtz's most serious transgression was: "He had taken a high seat among the devils of the land—I mean literally" (p. 116).

Kurtz carries the arrogant isolation of the colonialist to its extreme: he sets himself up as a god to be worshiped by the natives. Kurtz has no relations with other human beings but only with objects viewed as possessions. Marlow says, "Oh yes, I heard him. 'My Intended, my ivory, my station, my river, my'—everything belonged to him" (p. 116). When Marlow confronts Kurtz in the forest, he realizes that Kurtz is totally isolated morally. There is no standard or sentiment to which Marlow can appeal. Kurtz has "kicked himself loose of the earth. Confound the man! he had kicked the very earth to pieces" (p. 144).

In *Heart of Darkness* Conrad makes it clearer than in any of his other novels that benevolent and exploitative colonialism are really contiguous. Lingard, Jim, and Kurtz are all alike in living in a "world without men," and it is only a step from the unthinking harm done by the paternalist to the

81

conscious malice of the fiend. Kurtz himself began as "an emissary of pity, and science, and progress" (p. 79), but even from the start he placed himself metaphorically in the position of a god that he later was to assume literally. Marlow says of Kurtz's report to the International Society for the Suppression of Savage Customs: "The opening paragraph . . . in the light of later information, strikes me now as ominous. He began with the argument that we whites, from the point of development we had arrived at, 'must necessarily appear to them [savages] in the nature of supernatural beings—we approach them with the might as of a deity'" (p. 118). From the moment Kurtz became a colonialist, he left the world of others. Conrad plainly indicates here that he did not feel the original "civilizing mission" was noble had it only not been subverted by material lust. Rather the hubris of the "civilizers" paved the way for all that was to follow.

In his examination of the colonial situation, Conrad investigates the psychology of the natives as well as that of the colonialists. Compared with his remarkable analysis of the Europeans, Conrad's depiction of the natives is admittedly superficial. In his author's note to *A Personal Record* he excuses himself by saying, "Of course I don't know anything about Malays" (p. vi). His glimpses of native life must have been very brief and restricted because of his position as a mariner. Nonetheless, his understanding of natives was sufficient to draw praise from several modern third-world writers. D. C. R. A. Goonetilleke, a critic from Sri Lanka, has said of Conrad, "His Malayan world is predominantly authentic in all its varied spheres. . . . He is able to rise above conventional Western prejudices."[5] And the black South African critic Ezekiel Mphahlele has written, "The three outstanding white novelists who portray competently characters belonging to cultural groups outside their own are Josef Conrad, E. M. Forster, and William Faulkner."[6]

The subject of native psychology has occasioned much debate in our era of decolonization. In *Prospero and Caliban* O. Mannoni made the controversial claim that natives have a "dependency complex" that is reciprocal to the inferiority complex of the colonialists. The natives' dependency derives from their cult of the dead. In many African and Asian societies the dead ancestors are worshiped and thought to be governing the lives of the living. For all major decisions, the natives depend on the dead, who supposedly speak through signs, tongues, and oracles. When the colonialists appear, the natives, regarding them as supernatural because of their advanced technological power, include them along with the dead as persons to depend on. Thus if the colonialists can be said to be living in a "world without men," the natives exist in a magical and haunted world without solitude.

There is probably some truth in Mannoni's theory. In his essay "The Blacks," the black South African writer Peter Abrahams says: "What then is tribal man? Perhaps his most important single characteristic is that he is not an individual in the western sense. Psychologically and emotionally he is the present living personification of a number of forces, among the most important of which are the ancestral dead."[7] In his novel *Fragments*, published in 1970, the Ghanaian writer Ayi Kwei Armah makes use of the idea of dependence on the dead. He sees that dependence being transferred to the modern educated elite, typified by his hero, Baako. And in her study of modern Vietnam, *Fire in the Lake*, Frances Fitzgerald makes persuasive use of Mannoni's theory of the dependency complex.

Conrad's depiction of native psychology anticipates Mannoni in indicating the existence of a dependency complex. In his novels the Europeans Lingard, Jim, and Kurtz are all regarded by the natives, at least for a while, as supernatural.

They are all attributed with magical powers. In *An Outcast of the Islands* Ali thinks that "the Rajah Laut could make himself invisible. Also, he could be in two places at once" (p. 317). In *Lord Jim* the natives gifted Jim "with supernatural powers" and thought he carried the cannons "up the hill on his back—two at a time" (p. 266). In *Heart of Darkness* the natives regard Fresleven, Marlow's predecessor, as a "supernatural being" (p. 54) and flee their village in terror after he is accidentally killed. And the Africans farther up the river accept Kurtz as a god because, not understanding the mechanics of his rifles, they think he "came to them with thunder and lightning" (p. 128).

Part of the power of the whites is that they do not believe in the spirits, whereas the natives do. In Conrad's story "The Lagoon" (1897) the whites are seen as "unbelievers and in league with the Father of Evil, who leads them unharmed through the invisible dangers of this world" (p. 190). In *An Outcast of the Islands* Babalatchi says of Willems that "he, being white, cannot hear the voice of those that died" (p. 231). And in the story "Karain: A Memory" (1897) the title character flees to the whites because the spirit of the dead Pata Matara cannot follow him there: "You men with white faces who despise the invisible voices. He cannot abide your unbelief and your strength" (p. 24).

In several places in Conrad the whites are actually equated with the dead by the natives. In *Lord Jim* Jewel seems to regard both Jim and Marlow as "shades." Marlow says of Jewel's interrogation of him, "Thus a poor mortal seduced by the charm of an apparition might have tried to wring from another ghost the tremendous secret of the claim the other world holds over a disembodied soul astray amongst the passions of this earth" (p. 315). And in "Karain" the whites are regarded as having power over the dead. The amulet that Hollis makes from a Jubilee sixpence with the image of

Queen Victoria on it is sufficient to drive away Karain's ghostly nemesis.

Because of their lack of belief in spirits, the whites, unlike the natives, are alone. Karain refers to "your land of unbelief, where the dead do not speak, where every man is wise, and alone" (p. 44). This point is important because of the emphasis which Conrad places on existential solitude. It is with some condescension, and surprisingly little regret, that Conrad indicates the natives are not alone. Occasionally, however, they are privileged with glimpses of their own solitude. When Willems spurns Aissa, she becomes dejected "as if to her—to her, the savage, violent, and ignorant creature—had been revealed clearly in that moment the tremendous fact of our isolation" (*Outcast*, p. 250). And, after Omar dies, Babalatchi feels "for a moment the weight of his loneliness" and nearly utters a cry "as true, as great, as profound, as any philosophical shriek that ever came from the depths of an easy-chair to disturb the impure wilderness of chimneys and roofs." But, Conrad goes on to say, "for half a minute and no more did Babalatchi face the gods in the sublime privilege of his revolt, and then the one-eyed puller of wires became himself again . . . a victim of the tormenting superstitions of his race" (*Outcast*, pp. 214–15).

The most controversial aspect of Mannoni's theory of the dependency complex is his interpretation of anticolonial uprisings. Through a convoluted process of logic, he sees these uprisings resulting not from a genuine wish for freedom but from a fear of abandonment. Thus he notes that the 1947 rebellion in Madagascar took place immediately after the French instituted a series of liberal reforms. Supposedly the covert purpose of the rebellion was to reestablish a pattern of dependence, either by setting up charismatic indigeneous leaders or by provoking the French to reassert their authority (see pp. 132–41).

85

This aspect of Mannoni's theory has been attacked vehemently by the other most important modern investigator of colonial psychology, Frantz Fanon, a black psychiatrist from Martinique who joined the Algerian revolution. In his book *Black Skin, White Masks* Fanon accepts Mannoni's analysis of the colonialist, but he disagrees with the idea of a native dependency complex in the colonial situation. Referring to General Joseph-Simon Galliéni, the first French resident-general of the colony of Madagascar, Fanon attacks Mannoni by arguing: "After having sealed the Malagasy into his own customs, after having evolved a unilateral analysis of his view of the world, after having described the Malagasy within a closed circle, after having noted that the Malagasy has a dependency relation toward his ancestors—a strong tribal characteristic—M. Mannoni, in defiance of all objectivity, applies his conclusions to a bilateral totality—deliberately ignoring the fact that, since Galliéni, the Malagasy has ceased to exist."[8]

Fanon's point is that psychological mechanisms do not remain unchanged with the advent of colonialism. The natives are not dependent on the colonialists in exactly the same way as on the dead. After all, the colonialists are tangible, living men just like the natives—a fact that eventually becomes clear. With respect to the colonialists, the natives are slaves and their ultimate project will be to revolt. Whereas Mannoni believed native rebellions were caused by a fear of abandonment, Fanon saw them as a struggle for independence.

Joseph Conrad appears to agree with Fanon on this point. While the attack on Marlow's steamer by Kurtz's followers might possibly be interpreted as caused by a fear of abandonment, nearly all the rest of Conrad's natives transcend whatever dependency they may have on Europeans and enter into active revolt. Mrs. Almayer, Nina, Lakamba, Babalatchi,

Abdulla, Dain Maroola, Omar, Aissa, Gobila, Rajah Allang, Doramin, and Jewel all end up hating Europeans, and most have as their primary goal in life the expulsion of the colonialists from their lands. Conrad was himself a native of a country that had been colonized by Germany, Austria, and Russia, and as such he endorsed, with however tempered optimism, anticolonial revolts.[9] Only by such means could an end be put to the nightmarish subservience of the colonized and the solipsistic arrogance of the colonialists. At the close of "Karain" Jackson speaks for Conrad when he considers the possibility that the Mindanao chief whom he had befriended is now participating in an uprising against the Spanish in the Philippines: "I saw a paper this morning; they are fighting over there again. He's sure to be in it. He will make it hot for the caballeros. Well, good luck to him!" (p. 54).

Avrom Fleishman

The Landscape of Hysteria
in *The Secret Agent*

In the author's note to his recent novel, *The White Hotel*, the British poet D. M. Thomas describes his unusual subject with what he takes to be a familiar phrase. "One could not travel far in the landscape of hysteria," he begins, "the 'terrain' of this novel—without meeting of the majestic figure of Sigmund Freud. Freud becomes one of the dramatis personae, in fact, as discoverer of the great and beautiful modern myth of psychoanalysis."[1] Despite the popularity of this astonishing and, I venture to predict, enduring novel, perhaps a summary of its constituent elements is in order: a prologue consisting of fictional letters to and from Freud; a longish poem reciting the erotic fantasies of a woman undergoing psychoanalysis; the journal of a fantasized affair between the woman and Freud's son at a resort hotel, amid an international set reminiscent of *The Magic Mountain*; an extended imitation of a Freudian case history, perfectly capturing Freud's style, scientism, and humanity; a narrative, with intercalated letters, covering the heroine's life between the wars, up to her marriage to a Russian opera singer; the narrative of her martyrdom in the Holocaust, drawing heavily on the testimony of survivors; and finally, a visionary account of a passage to some promised land, some-

what resembling biblical and/or post-war Palestine, Dante's
Limbo, and other images of postmortal existence.

Even before I was absorbed, disturbed, repelled, and inspired (not necessarily in that order) by the events and emotions in Thomas's novel, I was struck by the words
"landscape of hysteria" in the first sentence of its preface. He
seemed to be using the phrase as an established critical term,
yet although I've been studying the subject of landscape and
townscape in literature and art for some time, I hadn't come
across that precise formulation before. Then in a book on
American literary townscape, by David R. Weimer, I came
upon it and began the series of speculations that follows.

Weimer uses the phrase "landscape of hysteria" to describe
the fictional world of Stephen Crane, both in the novel of
battlefield experience, *The Red Badge of Courage*, and in the
"naturalist" stories of the New York slums, "Maggie" and
"George's Mother." To quote Weimer's summary: "The illusions of the unheroic hero in *Red Badge* mirror 'the insanely
grotesque and incongruous world of battle into which he is
plunged,' and in *Maggie* there is a similar 'landscape of
hysteria'—a phrase that suggests beautifully Crane's matching of irrationalities in person and place."[2] For Weimer, this
mirroring and matching of outside and inside are crucial and
make Crane's fiction a metaphor or figurative expression of
the "*connectedness* of his characters with experience outside
themselves. For him, despite the immensity and imperson-
ality of war or the city, the objective world is knitted to the
subjective, is in a way its expression" (p. 63). (This accolade is
pronounced by contrast with the "sense of disconnectedness
. . . between characters and their environment" in Kafka,
whose "surrealist" universe is politely granted its place in the
sun but is nevertheless ascribed to extraliterary convictions,
"sexual or political or religious.")

Weimer is, in fact, drawing upon previous critical work for

the term "landscape of hysteria," and it may be worthwhile to follow the chain a link further back to see what the term has meant to others. Weimer's source is Charles C. Walcutt's book on American literary naturalism, and Walcutt's description of Crane responds to the hysteria of his world not metaphorically but literally. While suggesting that the hysteria is put in place by the author— "Crane's hallucinatory inferno is a gift of his style" (p. 60)—he also says that it's there in the subject-matter to begin with: "The hysterical distortions symbolize, image, and even dramatize the confusion of values which puts these social waifs in a moral madhouse."[3] In the tradition of criticism that sees form as the symbolic equivalent of content, Walcutt does not stop with the deplorable social scene and personal degradations that Crane witnesses, but specifies the stylistic techniques by which he conveys his "nightmarish world hovering between hallucination and hysteria": "violent verbs, distorted scenes, and sensory transfer." The verbs, such as "howling," "writhing," "convulsed," "raving," are remarkable enough; "sensory transfer" seems to refer to Crane's idiosyncratic application of color terms to abstract or nonvisual referents, for example, "red years," "yellow discontent." But for an idea of what Walcutt means by "distorted scenes," we had best return to Weimer's book for a close scenic analysis.

Commenting on a passage of Crane's story, "George's Mother," in which an oppressive urban scene is rendered from the point of view of—or, as a more recent theoretical terminology would put it, as focalized by—the title-character, Weimer sums up its effect: "This character is curiously responsive to her surroundings. She detects chimneys growing, laundry as strange leaves on vines, a brewery as a monstrous bird and then [as] a machine, grime as an enemy. The strangeness in the world about her is also her strangeness. Because it remains ambiguous . . . whether the perceiving mind is the character's or Crane's, we cannot say certainly that the queerness exits only in her mind or only in her surroundings. For Crane it seems present in both, almost indistinguishably."[4]

When we reexamine the passages of "George's Mother" on which Weimer's summary is based, Crane's specific techniques for achieving continuity between "strangeness in the world" and the strangeness of the perceiving mind become clearer. We find, to be sure, the regular shifting of point-of-view or "focalization" that Weimer mentions:

> She looked out at chimneys growing thickly on the roofs. A man at work on one seemed like a bee. In the intricate yards below, vine-like lines had strange leaves of cloth. To her ears there came the howl of the man with the red, mottled face. He was engaged in a furious altercation with the youth who had called attention to his poor aim. They were like animals in a jungle. In the distance an enormous brewery towered over the other buildings. Great gilt letters advertised a brand of beer. Thick smoke came from funnels and spread near it like vast and powerful wings. The structure seemed a great bird, flying. The letters of the sign made a chain of gold hanging from its neck. The little old woman looked at the brewery. It vaguely interested her, for a moment, as a stupendous affair, a machine of mighty strength.[5]

The clear indications of perspective — "She looked out at chimneys," "To her ears there came the howl," and so on — are intercalated with other sentences in which the authority for perception can be only arguably assigned: "A man at work on one seemed like a bee"; "They were like animals in a jungle." As we are unable infallibly to distinguish the so-called omniscient narration from the character's point-of-view, sentence by sentence, the effect of perspectival ambiguity or indistinguishability of inner and outer worlds of which Weimer speaks certainly occurs. But I would note another verbal impulse of even greater influence, the semantic chain formed by metaphors and similes, almost uniformly distributed one to a sentence: "chimneys growing thickly," "seemed like a bee," "vine-like lines," "howl of the man" (not inevitably metaphoric, but here laden with bestial associations), "animals in a jungle," and so on. Whether we attend to this sequence primarily for its stylistic consistency or for its referential accumulation—that is, whether foregrounding the prevalence of metaphors or the imaged world of primitive nature they produce—we are made aware of a unifying power that sweeps up character and environment alike. This power is Crane's figurative language, stronger than external poverty, stronger than psychic distortion, in its ability to break down the strict demarcations of subjectivity and objectivity and to fashion a consistent fictional world, the landscape of hysteria.

I know that these remarks tread precariously near tautology, for they might be reduced to the view that since writing is inevitably at least partially figurative, even when it aims to be literal, any novelistic treatment of place is a mixture of metaphor and denotation. Yet before surrendering to this seductive simplification, it may be possible to distinguish other modes of achieving such fusions of personal and worldly hysteria. Crane's mode is predominantly metaphoric, but his is not the only option. Although all fictional language—and perhaps language in general—is metaphoric at bottom, some fictional texts not only purport to deliver literal descriptions of imagined objects or events, but employ literal language as systematically and effectively as Crane employs metaphor. We may perhaps usefully compare some instances of stylistic literalism to see how *its* landscapes— especially landscapes of hysteria—differ from the metaphoric ones of writers like Crane. Let us check in again at *The White Hotel*.

As the previous summary or other reviews of the novel may have suggested, Thomas, too, works by juxtaposing the metaphoric and the literal, the subjective and the objective. The novelist first sets out the elementary images of a woman's mind, then rearranges them as they might be ordered, interpreted, mythified by psychoanalysis (he speaks of Freudianism as "myth, I mean a poetic, dramatic expression of a hidden truth"). Later these same images are literally enacted in a system of historical events, so that we are led to question our easy distinctions between private imaginings and public facts. Finally, the novel recycles some of these images as elements of another system, where we cannot be sure whether they are parts of a subjective world or of real, postmortal existence. I shall restrict myself to the interplay of the second and third stages of these images, as I'm not inclined to venture into the metaphysical questions raised by the first or final ones.

In the chapter of *The White Hotel* devoted to imitating the ideas and style of Freud's case studies, the fictional psychoanalyst writes of his patient's hysterical symptoms, pains in her chest and pelvic region:

> While I was thus dwelling on the universal aspect of Frau Anna's condition, Eros in combat with Thanatos, I stumbled over the root of her personal anguish. I had, up to this point, never been able to establish any particular event which might have been instrumental in unleashing her hysteria. The pains in her breast and ovary had attacked her at a time when she was busy and happy, successful in her resumed career, and eagerly anticipating her husband's first leave [from service in World War I], confident that all would now be well. . . . She had gone to bed quite happily one night, after writing her

husband a very affectionate letter hinting that she would like to become pregnant during his forthcoming leave. The pains had woken her that same night.[6]

There follows an account of the patient's revelation of traumatic childhood experiences, by means of which the analyst educes the symbolic valences of her images of her own breast and her mother's, her desire for impregnation and her negativity to sex following her mother's past indiscretions with a brother-in-law, her load of associations with a silver crucifix that her aunt had owned and the patient now wears, and her habit of stroking the cross during the ongoing analysis. When Freud points out its gestural significances, not all of which I can enlarge upon here, a watershed is reached: "My explanation had the effect of bringing back her fierce pains, but also of recalling to her mind a host of forgotten memories . . . and thence to untying the knot of her hysteria" (p. 132). Her observation of the primal scene involved the sight of mother *sans* crucifix: "Her fragile sense of her own worth had been sustained by the ikon of her mother's goodness. One flaw and it would shatter, shattering the young woman too." Her mother engaged in what the patient thinks of as incest, "did not wear a crucifix because she did not deserve to wear one. . . . Then instantly another thought—she, Anna, did not deserve to wear it either; she too should rip it from her neck" (p. 134).

Not all the significances of this passage are clear, if only because they aren't at all clear to the patient in her psychoanalysis—although the fictional Freud expresses considerable satisfaction in his explanation and in his judgment of the state of her psychic economy: "For every gift has its cost, and the price of freedom from intolerable knowledge had been an hysteria. . . . A few hours later, her pains came on. . . . But the price was worth paying; for the alternative would have been still worse" (p. 136). So the heroine continues on her battered way through life, the life of Europe between the wars, until she closes her earthly passage on the surface layer of a deep pit of bodies at the extermination center near Kiev known as Babi Yar:

> Then she heard people walking near her, actually on the bodies. They were Germans who had climbed down and were bending over and taking things from the dead and occasionally firing at those who showed signs of life.
>
> An SS man bent over an old woman lying on her side [that is, Anna], having seen a glint of something bright. His hand brushed her breast when he reached for the crucifix to pull it free, and he must have sensed a flicker of life. Letting go the crucifix he stood up. He drew his leg back and sent his jackboot crashing into her left breast. She moved position from the force of the blow, but uttered no sound. Still not satisfied, he swung his boot again and sent it cracking into her pelvis. Again the only sound was the clean snap of the bone. Satisfied at last, he jerked the crucifix free. He went off, picking his way across the corpses. (pp. 248–49)

This is surely the low point in the landscape of hysteria, but we must be careful to control our own tendencies toward that state when contemplating such a subject. As neutrally as we can, we may say that hysteria has ceased to be a state of mind and has become a fundamental condition of existence. To use the terms we have been employing: the subjectively figurative or mentally symptomatic has become the literal here—with a vengeance. More precisely, a metaphoric translation of a character's symbolic system (that is, the Freudian case study) has been superseded by another kind of text, a literalistic narrative imitating the matter-of-fact language of the eye-witness testimony of Dina Pronicheva, recounted in Anatoli Kuznetsov's *Babi Yar* (as the author's acknowledgment informs us).

Among the heavy implications we are to take away is this, that the distinction we are fond of maintaining between the objective and the subjective is no more resolutely fixed than the distinction between irrational states of mind and the irrationality of certain events in modern history. Not that there is *no* distinction — otherwise there would be no point to Thomas's elaborate juxtaposition — but the two run into each other; subjective hysteria is discovered to be an entirely accurate predictive index of objective experience.

There are other possible variations on the relationship between inner and outer hysteria, and — on the principle that the widest explorer of possibilities deserves title to a domain — I wish to assign Joseph Conrad a new and perhaps not entirely laudatory epithet, after all the others by which he's been designated: grand master of the landscape of hysteria. If this were only a way of referring to the grisly proceedings in his political novels and the somewhat stagy flashing of knives in his island tales, the epithet would merely echo the disturbed tones of his earliest reviewers and would thus be best left unsaid. But when ranged against the stylistic procedures of contemporary and later novelists, Conrad's methods of portraying the landscape of hysteria will be found among the most evocative and fruitful, and he thereby claims attention at a significant turning in the fictional tradition. The techniques that I have been considering — the alternating of omniscient and focalized narration, the mingling of figurative and literal stylistic modes, the juxtaposing of the horrors of hysterical neurosis and the sometimes greater horrors of the historical world — all find their place in such novels as *The Secret Agent*, and Conrad's varied ways of dealing with them make up a poetics of the fiction characteristic of this century.

I would begin with a text that has already received ample scrutiny in Conrad studies: the opening pages of chapter 2 of *The Secret Agent*, in which the secret agent Verloc makes his

way through the West End of London en route to an interview at a foreign embassy that sets in motion a pseudoanarch-
ist bombing at the Greenwich Observatory. Here, as in
Stephen Crane, a character's point-of-view is carefully established, only to give way recurrently to narrative observations
that read like those of a more elevated observer, or are at best
ambiguous in origin:

> Through the park railings [Verloc's] glances beheld men and
> women riding in the Row, couples cantering past harmo-
> niously, others advancing sedately at a walk, loitering groups
> of three or four, solitary horsemen looking unsociable, and
> solitary women followed at a long distance by a groom with a
> cockade to his hat and a leather belt over his tight-fitting coat.
> Carriages went bowling by, mostly two-horse broughams,
> with here and there a victoria with the skin of some wild beast
> inside and a woman's face and hat emerging above the folded
> hood. And a peculiarly London sun—against which nothing
> could be said except that it looked bloodshot—glorified all
> this by its stare. It hung at a moderate elevation above Hyde
> Park Corner with an air of punctual and benign vigilance.
> The very pavement under Mr. Verloc's feet had an old-gold
> tinge in that diffused light, in which neither wall, nor tree, nor
> beast, nor man cast a shadow. Mr. Verloc was going westward
> through a town without shadows in an atmoshpere of
> powdered old gold.[7]

The scene (of which I have quoted only part) is built up in a
manner that closely resembles Crane's: the steady march of
denotative units as the observer, Verloc, steadily marches
through the park; the addition of a number of metaphoric
expressions—a sun that "looked bloodshot," a pavement
with an "old-gold tinge" that broadens into "an atmosphere
of powdered old gold"—expressions that may correspond to
the visual sensations of the observer but are less likely to be

his own formulations than to be those of an omniscient narrator; and in the midst of this assemblage of a figurative version of an ordinary London scene, the careful placement of a distinct detail in sharply reduced, literal terms: a woman in a carriage covered not by the cultural artifact, furs, but by "the skin of some wild beast." The banality of the subjective observer is matched by the banality of the objects surrounding him; even a single qualitative adjective, "bloodshot," can refer both to the external world and to the observer's vision (the early-rising Verloc is likely to be bleary-eyed at this point). Around the accumulated detail of ordinary urban life, the suffused light of the overcast sun acts as a cohesive medium, visually and/or figuratively coating the entire field by the narrative equivalent of the painterly effect known as tonality. Ambiguities and juxtapositions do not create violent contrasts here, but instead raise hints of instability and hysteria within a scene that composes a serene accord between the observer and his world.

In the closing chapter of *The Secret Agent*, an esthetic effect closer to that of *The White Hotel* is achieved. As the parasitic anarchist Ossipon and the mad terrorist called "the Professor" review the denouement of the Greenwich bombing, Ossipon's mind repeatedly reverts to remembered phrases from a newspaper account of the suicide of one of the victims of the affair, Verloc's wife Winnie. Throughout the closing five pages of the novel, these phrases provide an insistent rhythm, resembling that of a ground or figured bass in music: "*An impenetrable mystery seems destined to hang for ever,*" "*An impenetrable mystery,*" "*To hang for ever over,*" "*This act of madness or despair,*" "*mystery destined to hang for ever,*" "*An impenetrable mystery is destined to hang for ever,*" "*An impenetrable mystery,*" "*This act of madness or despair,*" "*This act of madness or despair,*" "*Will hang for ever over this act,*" "*of madness or despair,*" "*An impenetrable mystery,*" "*This act of madness or despair*" (pp. 307–11). Here the uncanny mingling of the coldly objective and the wildly subjective, the impersonal journalistic report and the disturbed psychic fixation on the phrase, does not derive from the juxtaposing of one section of a text with another, as in Thomas's novel, but from line to line within a single section.

The effect of this rapid alternation is somewhat different from a simpler one earlier in *The Secret Agent*, when Winnie Verloc herself is unsettled by the remembered phrases of a newspaper account of a recent hanging. The iterative phrase, "The drop given was fourteen feet," acts as a direct stimulus to Winnie's fear of punishment for the murder of her husband, which she has just committed. The literalistic terms of the journalistic formula serve to reduce Winnie to hysteria, flight, and ultimately suicide. But in the final chapter, the interplay between psychic disturbance and external violence follows a more complicated program. We find the same frenzy being generated by the objective phrases of the newspaper report, but we also note the reverse movement—from subjectivity to objectivity (or something like it) taking place as well: Ossipon thinks himself "menaced by this thing in the very sources of his existence. He could not issue forth to meet his various [paramours] without the dread of beginning to talk to them of an impenetrable mystery destined. . . . He was becoming scientifically afraid of insanity lying in wait for him amongst these lines" (p. 307). Here the omniscient narrator's sardonic echoing of his character's naïve devotion to science serves a function similar to Thomas's prosaic report of history's atrocities against the suffering neurotic. In both texts, literal language serves to reduce the personal realm to absurdity, to *dreck* (in the current jargon), while at the same time standing as an objectification, a public demonstration, as it were, of personal hysteria.

The Landscape of Hysteria in The Secret Agent

If the transactions between inner and outer landscapes of hysteria, and between the metaphoric and the literal modes of portraying them, are characteristically manifold in Conrad, another passage of *The Secret Agent* stands as a high-water mark for the entire tradition of such landscapes. In chapter 8, coming at about midpoint in the text and serving as a moment of suspension (indeed, a narrative analepsis) in the inexorable unfolding of the plot, Winnie's mother is conveyed to an old-age home in a vehicle that comes to be called the Cab of Death. The rhetorical and allusive means by which Conrad develops the prosaic and faintly comic horse, cab, and cabman into symbols of the human condition have been widely acknowledged and well studied. I shall add only a few notes to this collective wisdom, focusing mainly on the means by which states of mind and external phenomena are yoked together to produce perhaps the most impressive of landscapes of hysteria:

> In the narrow streets the progress of the journey was made sensible to those within by the near fronts of the houses gliding past slowly and shakily, with a great rattle and jingling of glass, as if about to collapse behind the cab. . . . Later on, in the wider space of Whitehall, all visual evidences of motion became imperceptible. The rattle and jingle of glass went on indefinitely in front of the long Treasury building — and time itself seemed to stand still. . . . And for a time the walls of [Parliament], with its towers and pinnacles, contemplated in immobility and silence a cab that jingled. (pp. 156–57)

What begins as a close recording of subjective experience — time and space as measured from the limited perspective of the cab riders, using variable reference points — becomes, after a time, an objective and external view of them and their cab as seen from a lofty perspective, the heights of the Parliament building, yet without losing its poignant subjectivity, its plangent jingle.

The state of mind that I shall follow through this scene is that of Stevie, the mentally defective brother of Winnie Verloc, who is later induced to carry a package for his brother-in-law that shatters him into butcher's meat. On the present occasion, Stevie protests against a minor piece of butchery, the cabman's whipping of his sorry nag of a horse:

> "You mustn't," stammered out Stevie, violently, "it hurts."
>
> "Mustn't whip?" queried the other in a thoughtful whisper, and immediately whipped. He did this, not because his soul was cruel and his heart evil, but because he had to earn his fare. And for a time the walls of [Parliament], with its towers and pinnacles, contemplated in immobility and silence a cab that jingled. (p. 157)

The symbolic values are deftly laid down here for further elaboration in what follows: the cabman as mankind fated to labor by the sweat of its brow for meager reward and grotesque degradation; Stevie as incoherent protestor against pain and poverty, both human and animal; the elements of the London townscape as blank and indifferent to the human drama — although ironically said to contemplate it "in immobility and silence."

As the ride continues, however, these participants are elaborated by narrative details, many of which are impossible to assign exclusively either to the literal or the metaphoric realm. The cabman's fare of a few "pieces of silver," his declaration that "this ain't an easy world," the departing image of "the short, thick man limping busily, with the horse's head held aloft in his fist, the lank animal walking in stiff and forlorn dignity" are touches of realistic description that inevitably resonate with symbolic suggestion, reinforcing the earlier designations of the cabman as the Dionysian wisdom-figure Silenus and the horse as "the steed of apocalyptic misery" (pp. 167–68). The omniscient narration is not content to alternate between literal and figurative in its descriptive passages but self-consciously mingles them in certain sentences: Stevie "could say nothing; for the tenderness to all pain and all misery, the desire to make the horse happy and the cabman happy, had reached the point of a bizarre longing to take them to bed with him. And that, he knew, was impossible. For Stevie was not mad. It was, as it were, a symbolic longing; and at the same time it was very distinct, because springing from experience, the mother of wisdom" (p. 167). Just as Conrad's writing employs both modes of depiction, his character himself is said to mingle literal and figurative ideas: Stevie is aware of practical impossibilities but maintains "symbolic" longings. Finally, this passage of circumstantial psychological explanation for Stevie's disturbed ideas closes elegantly with a traditional metaphorical expression, "experience, the mother of wisdom."

I suspect that these observations will be readily accepted, for they don't go much beyond the established wisdom on Conrad. But my next point will be more difficult to make, for it can be fully established only be examining other passages of *The Secret Agent* and of the Conrad canon that lie beyond the scope of this essay. The point must be expressed baldly if it's to be made at all, but my apology must be that its violence is Conrad's and not my own. The point is threefold: the literal character, Stevie, in the paragraph after the cabman's withdrawal, becomes a figure of Charity; his charity, perhaps all charity, is precisely defined as a compound of love and hate; finally, this complex of literal and symbolic terms is raised to thematic relevance by association with revolutionary movements, of which the anarchists in the novel provide only a sham, satirically reduced version. My evidence lies in the following paragraph:

> Stevie[,] left alone beside the private lamp-post of the Charity [the public old-age home at which his mother has been deposited], his hands thrust deep into his pockets, glared with vacant sulkiness. At the bottom of his pockets his incapable, weak hands were clinched hard into a pair of angry fists. In the face of anything which affected directly or indirectly his morbid dread of pain, Stevie ended by turning vicious. A magnanimous indignation swelled his frail chest to bursting, and caused his candid eyes to squint. Supremely wise in knowing his own powerlessness, Stevie was not wise enough to restrain his passions. The tenderness of his universal charity had two phases as indissolubly joined and connected as the reverse and obverse sides of a medal. The anguish of immoderate compassion was succeeded by the pain of an innocent but pitiless rage. Those two states expressing themselves outwardly by the same signs of futile bodily agitation, his sister Winnie soothed his excitement without ever fathoming its twofold character. (pp. 168–69)

If we are willing to see Stevie standing under the sign of Charity not only literally but symbolically, and if we are willing to extend the psychological account of his mixed passions of love and hate to what we know from other Conrad novels of revolution, like *Nostromo, Under Western Eyes*, and *The Rover*, then we may be able to take Stevie as both a literal and symbolic figure of Revolution. By contrast, the anarchists of *The Secret Agent*, who are shown to lack love in any perceptible degree, can be no revolutionaries—they are too simple for that, merely hating and being hateful as they are. Winnie, too, is simple, and the text at hand stresses her contrast with her brother: "Winnie soothed his excitement without ever fathoming its twofold character." Here the literal character, expanded to symbolic dimensions, becomes a point of reference by which other characters and themes come to be real.

Something of the same duplexity must impress us as lying in the essence of Conradian landscape, whether in the primal forests of *Heart of Darkness* or in the swarming modern townscape of *The Secret Agent*. The landscape of hysteria is built up in these scenes neither as a decadent external world impinging on the protagonists' consciousness, nor as a phantasmal projection of personal disturbance upon a neutral nature or an indifferent social world, but as a fusion of the two, where it is no longer possible fully to distinguish inner and outer contributions. Conrad's mixture of literal and metaphoric technique is both the expressive medium of this fusion and—we may speculate—a calculated position on the nature of modern political violence, where inner and outer, literal and psychic horror are indistinguishable.

H. M. Daleski

Victory and Patterns
of Self-Division

Virtually the sole interest of *Victory*, given the absence in the novel of the characteristic Conradian virtues, is the presentation of Heyst. The main action is melodramatic rather than epiphanic, the narrative method is arbitrarily inconsistent rather than intricately functional, the language is frequently flat or rhetorical, and the characterization of most of the figures surrounding Heyst hovers between the crudity of caricature and the bluntness of allegory—but Heyst himself has the distinctive complexity of being which graces more memorable characters in Conrad's earlier and better work. Heyst, indeed, is so complex that Conrad criticism is full of contradictory statements about him. On the one hand, the detachment of this "man of universal detachment," as the novelist himself describes him in his 1920 author's note,[1] is held by some critics to be no more than a "pose"[2] or an "adopted role";[3] it is also said to be "unnatural"[4] and, insofar as it reflects "his father's angry scepticism," to be "alien to his temperament."[5] On the other hand, it is asserted that Heyst's detachment is so deeply part of him as to be incapacitating: he is said to exhibit "an inability to act or to love,"[6] an "incapacity . . . for love,"[7] and an "incapacity to act;"[8] where he does show pity, this is deemed to be "suspect."[9]

There is no need of a deconstructionist analysis in order to see how the text has given rise to such contradictory views, for they seem to thrust themselves at us. If it is intimated that Heyst is fundamentally a man of detachment since we are told that it is "the very essence of his life to be a solitary achievement, accomplished . . . by the detachment of an impermanent dweller amongst changing scenes" (p. 90) and, furthermore, that he is "temperamentally . . . a spectator" (p. 185), it is also categorically stated that he is "temperamentally sympathetic" (p. 70). It would seem to be clear, therefore, that Heyst is temperamentally prone both to a solitary detachment and a sympathetic involvement with others, and so it is misleading to conclude that only one of these opposed tendencies is genuine.[10] The personality that is presented to us is essentially dualistic in nature, and it is striking that the opening sentences of the novel should advert us to a notion of duality: "There is, as every schoolboy knows in this scientific age, a very close chemical relation between coal and diamonds. It is the reason, I believe, why some people allude to coal as 'black diamonds'" (p. 3). These statements recall D. H. Lawrence's use of a similar image to convey his sense of the duality of being and of the "allotropic states" which the individual "passes through": "Like as diamond and coal are the same pure single element of carbon. The ordinary novel would trace the history of the diamond—but I say, 'Diamond, what! This is carbon.' And my diamond might be coal or soot, and my theme is carbon." *The Rainbow*, which exemplifies Lawrence's apprehension of the carbon of character, appeared in the same year as *Victory*, but its central impetus is toward the integration of the dualistic self, and consequently it does not throw much light on Conrad's novel. *Victory* is illuminated, rather, by a number of nineteenth-century novels that are concerned, as I shall argue Conrad is in this work, with self-division. This is not to suggest that the novels I have in mind—Emily Brontë's *Wuthering Heights*, George Eliot's *The Mill on the Floss*, and Thomas Hardy's *Jude the Obscure*—should be regarded as having directly influenced Conrad, but merely that the patterns of self-division they present are close enough to the configurations of *Victory* to help us clarify its difficulties.[11]

In these nineteenth-century novels the two main opposed forces within the protagonists are concretized in two characters with whom they are each brought into close relationship. Thus in *Wuthering Heights* the animal-like wildness of Heathcliff is set against the refined cultivation of Edgar Linton, and the two men may be regarded as embodying opposed tendencies within Catherine Earnshaw, who is drawn to both of them. In *The Mill on the Floss* the intellectuality of Philip Wakem is set against the sexuality of Stephen Guest, and the opposition between them projects the self-division of Maggie Tulliver, who is torn between them. In *Jude the Obscure* Arabella Donn is portrayed as "a complete and substantial female animal—no more, no less," while Sue Bridehead is said to be "so uncarnate" that "her spirit" may be seen "trembling through her limbs," and the opposition between them reflects the conflict between flesh and spirit within Jude Fawley, who moves back and forth between the two women. In *Victory* the central relationships are not patterned in a love triangle as in the nineteenth-century novels, but they do take the form of a triangle, and it seems to me that Heyst's self-division is projected in an analogous manner: the doctrine of detachment propounded by his father is set against an instinctive capacity for attachment in Lena, and the opposition within Heyst between urges to detachment and attachment is figured in his strong feeling for both his father and the young woman.

When he leaves school at the age of eighteen, Heyst lives with his father for three years, and since the father is an epitome of "disillusion and regret," we are told that "such companionship at that plastic and impressionable age" could not but "leave in the boy a profound mistrust of life" (p. 91). The father's influence, indeed, is deadly, as is first suggested when, during their last talk together before the elder Heyst dies, the very houses in the moonlit London street begin to look to the son "like the tombs of an unvisited, unhonoured cemetery of hopes." The father's final exhortation to his son on this occasion is: "Look on—make no sound"; but since he recognizes that the boy may not yet be capable of so perfect a detachment, he advises him "to cultivate that form of contempt which is called pity" as a preliminary to the attainment of "a full and equable contempt" which will do away with all belief in "flesh and blood" (pp. 174–75). It is one of the ironies of this injunction that pity is not only a form of contempt but also of compassion, and that if Heyst doggedly seeks to "sustain" himself on contempt (p. 177), it is his compassion that leads him to the more tangible sustenance of attachment. The immediate effect of the father's influence, however, is to turn him decisively against any such possibility:

> Great achievements are accomplished in a blessed, warm mental fog, which the pitiless cold blasts of the father's analysis had blown away from the son.
>
> "I'll drift," Heyst had said to himself deliberately.
>
> He did not mean intellectually or sentimentally or morally. He meant to drift altogether and literally, body and soul, like a detached leaf drifting in the wind-currents under the immovable trees of a forest glade; to drift without ever catching on to anything.
>
> "This shall be my defence against life," he had said to

himself with a sort of inward consciousness that for the son of his father there was no other worthy alternative. (p. 92)

The "pitiless cold blasts of the father's analysis" may have the salutary effect of dissipating all "mental fog" in his son, but it is evident that they also detach the leaf from the tree and leave it to drift in the wind. The fallen leaf is no doubt a vivid image of detachment, but it has a number of subversive undertones. To drift is to lack purposive direction, and in Conrad from as early as *The Nigger of the "Narcissus"* drift is associated with a general meaninglessness. A drifting leaf, moreover, is vulnerable as a defensive posture since it may be presumed to be at the mercy of every breeze. Most damagingly of all, the detached leaf is a dying leaf, cut off from that which might sustain it, removed, as it were, from the body of life — and in a related image Heyst is on another occasion said to be "like a feather floating lightly in the work-a-day atmosphere" (p. 60).

The father's influence on his son is thus clearly pernicious, but it is misleading to regard the view of life which Heyst holds to as having been imposed on him or adopted as an affectation. After his father's death he proceeds to drift for some fifteen years, and this would seem to indicate that something already deep in himself was merely reinforced by his father's directives. The point may perhaps be clarified by reference to what happens to the young Cathy Earnshaw when she first leaves Wuthering Heights and spends some time at Thrushcross Grange. The "wild . . . little savage" who left the Heights returns to it "a lady," and Nelly Dean is quick to conclude that her refinement is a pose, deliberately adopted for her own devious purposes. It is evident, however, that the Grange only fosters and develops what is from the outset potential in Cathy. Nelly believes that Cathy simply conceals what she (Nelly) calls "her rough side," and that this is the real Cathy, but what we might call her smooth side is every bit as much part of her. Similarly, when Heyst says of himself that he is "a man of universal scorn and unbelief," and Lena accuses him of "putting it on," he replies: "No. I am like that, born or fashioned, or both" (p. 199); and we realize, with him, that his father has merely drawn out what is inherent in him. His drifting like a detached leaf for fifteen years suggests he is driven by an inner compulsion. Just what it is that drives him is intimated by his adoption of this mode of being as a "defence against life." That he feels the need to defend himself implies a general fear of life, and he certainly envisages life in threatening terms: "I often asked myself, with a momentary dread," he tells Lena, "in what way would life try to get hold of me?" (p. 202). It is for this reason that he insists so strenuously on emulating a detached leaf, adjuring all connection. "I only know," he says to her too, "that he who forms a tie is lost"; and though he explains this pronouncement by referring to "the germ of corruption" which then enters the soul (pp. 200–201), the language he uses suggests his specific fear is a fear of giving himself to another—of the loss of self such giving may be deemed to entail.

Where Heyst's father typifies the disengagement of a position of detachment, Lena figures the embrace of attachment. She it is, when Heyst shows a compassionate interest in her, who flings herself into his arms (p. 83), as she readily admits: "You took me up from pity," she tells him. "I threw myself at you" (p. 354). For her the embrace of love is both a *raison d'être* — "She thought . . . that she would try to hold him as long as she could—till her fainting arms, her sinking soul, could cling to him no more" (p. 246) — and the emblem of her being: "He bent down and took her under the arms, raising her straight out of the chair into a sudden and close embrace. Her alacrity to respond, which made her seem as light as a feather, warmed his heart at that moment more than closer caresses had done before. He had not expected that ready impulse towards himself which had been dormant in her passive attitude" (p. 223).

It is notable that the feather image should recur in this passage, for in its evocation of a light alacrity of response it is set against the floating feather of Heyst's unaccommodating and unaccommodated detachment. Where the influence of Heyst's father is deathly in effect, moreover, Lena's responsiveness is heartwarming, a force for life. Where the father teaches the young man to reflect, which, we are assumed, is "a destructive process" (p. 91), unleashing icy blasts, Lena instructs him in the hidden power of a sudden spontaneity, for her "ready impulse" has been "dormant in her passive attitude," and this, as it warms him, is restorative. Lena's very sense of self seems to inhere in a ready acceptance of connection: "Do you know," she says to Heyst, "it seems to me, somehow, that if you were to stop thinking of me I shouldn't be in the world at all!" (p. 187).

Attachment may thus be viewed as leading to the establishment of self, but this would appear to be dependent on a readiness to lose the self. Certainly Lena's willingness in this respect is repeatedly indicated: we are told, for instance, that whenever she speaks to him she seems "to abandon to him something of herself" (p. 188); and that she feels "in her innermost depths an irresistible desire to give herself up to him more completely, by some act of absolute sacrifice" (p. 201). A capacity for such abandon, moreover, is not only in contrast to the tight withholding of self that characterizes the posture of detachment; it is also, in its courageous audacity, set against the fear that underlies the withholding: the expression on Lena's face when Heyst first meets her is said to have in it "something indefinably audacious and infinitely miserable — because the temperament and the existence of that girl [are] reflected in it" (p. 74); and Lena at once demonstrates her audacity in insisting that Heyst accept the responsibility of his interest in her: "*You* do something," she says to him. "You are a gentleman. It wasn't I who spoke to you first, was it? I didn't begin, did I? It was you who came along and spoke to me when I was standing over there. What did you want to speak to me for? I don't care what it is, but you must do something" (p. 80). The courage to give the self is also, in its concomitant trustfulness, posed against that "profound mistrust of life" which both breeds and epitomizes detachment: "He could not believe that the creature he had coveted with so much force and with so little effect, was in reality tender, docile to her impulses, and had almost offered herself to [him] without a sense of guilt, in a desire of safety, and from a profound need of placing her trust where her woman's instinct guided her ignorance" (p. 95).

Heyst's own readiness for attachment, like his inclination to detachment, issues from his deepest being. "There must be a lot of the original Adam in me, after all," he reflects, and the nature of the old Adam in him is implicitly defined not as inherent evil but as a compulsion to bring himself into relation with his circumambient world: "There was in the son a lot of that first ancestor who, as soon as he could uplift his muddy frame from the celestial mould, started inspecting and naming the animals of that paradise which he was so soon to lose" (pp. 173–74). The old Adam repeatedly and incongruously declares itself in the proclaimed solitary, for if he wanders the world alone, he is also "a ready letter-writer," and during his wandering writes "pages and pages" about his experiences to "his friends in Europe," so it is said (p. 6). Nor does he always withdraw from more direct contact. On the contrary, when business brings him to Sourabaya, he seems to be naturally gregarious, being rash enough, for instance, quite gratuitously to invite the notorious Mr. McNab to "come along and quench [his] thirst" with him (p. 8). But it is, of course, in relation to Morrison that he first conclusively gives way to an instinctive and spontaneous fellow-feeling — and invites the attachment that changes the course of his life.

The occasion of Heyst's involvement with Morrison, indeed, is the attachment of the latter's brig by Portuguese officials in Delli. What is notable about his encounter with Morrison is the way in which Heyst involves himself with him when there is no apparent need to do so. He is a "stranger" to Morrison (p. 15), and anyway Morrison does not even see him: when they meet, Morrison is "walking along the street, his eyeglass tossed over his shoulder, his head down, with the hopeless aspect of those hardened tramps one sees . . . trudging from workhouse to workhouse," and it is only when he is hailed from across the street by Heyst that he looks up "with a wild worried expression" (p. 12). Heyst's response is to invite Morrison to join him for a drink, and then, when he discovers the trouble he is in, to offer him a loan that will enable him to get his brig back. Heyst acts on his impulses, being directed by a strong feeling of compassion for Morrison, not contempt, and his action has far-reaching implications, for he is later said to have "plunged after the submerged Morrison" (p. 77). The image of the plunge, in its evocation of generous abandon, suggests that this man, who fears a loss of self, is also capable of risking the self, for it is after a "submerged" man that he plunges, pursuing a rescue by means of attachment.

In *Wuthering Heights, The Mill on the Floss,* and *Jude the Obscure,* the clash of conflicting qualities within the central protagonists is sharpened and pointed by the active rivalry of the two characters who in each case embody the opposed qualities. Thus Heathcliff and Edgar, Philip and Stephen, and Arabella and Sue are all brought in one way or another in direct, usually hostile, confrontation. In *Victory* Heyst's father is long dead before his son even meets Lena, but the opposition between them, the battle for Heyst that is implicitly waged, is nonetheless central to the main action. The death of the father if anything intensifies his influence: "A few slow tears rolled down [Heyst's] face. The rooms, filling with shadows, seemed haunted by a melancholy, uneasy presence which could not express itself. The young man got up with a strange sense of making way for something impalpable that claimed possession, went out of the house, and locked the door. A fortnight later he started on his travels—to 'look on and never make a sound'" (p. 176). It is not of the house alone that the spirit of Heyst's father "claims possession," nor only those rooms which from this point on are haunted by the "melancholy, uneasy presence." The "something impalpable" takes a more palpable form in the attitudes and pronouncements of the son who is possessed. It is in this respect that Conrad may be regarded as moving beyond the three nineteenth-century novelists and sounding a characteristic modern note. There is little indication in their work of the source of the split in their protagonists; Conrad, with a Freudian-like awareness, makes us see Heyst as a man who carries his family ghosts with him.

The elder Heyst also inhabits the possessions that he leaves to his son. Heyst eventually brings these to his island retreat—"a lot of books, some chairs and tables, his father's portrait in oils . . . [and] a lot of small objects"; and we are told that it is "their presence there which [attaches] him to the island" when he wakes up to "the failure of his apostasy" (p. 177). When Lena comes to the island, she finds the main room of their house "lined with the backs of books halfway up on its three sides. . . . In the dusk and coolness nothing [gleams] except the gilt frame of the portrait of Heyst's father, signed by a famous painter, lonely in the middle of a wall" (p. 168). And the elder Heyst is an active ghost: when his son reads one of the books his father has written, "shrinking into himself, composing his face as if under the author's eye, with a vivid consciousness of the portrait on his right hand, a little above his head, a wonderful presence in its heavy frame on the flimsy wall of mats," he seems to hear his father's voice, and half believes that "something of his father [dwells] yet on earth—a ghostly voice, audible to the ear of his own flesh and blood" (pp. 218–19).

The elder Heyst, however, is not the only ghost with a claim on the son's attention. When Lena comes out to Heyst in the garden of the hotel, it is a "white, phantom-like apparition" that he sees and which proceeds to cling to him (p. 83); and a little later he again registers that, "white and spectral, she [is] putting out her arms to him out of the black shadows like an appealing ghost" (p. 86). It is thus that Lena confronts Heyst's father, and she is often placed in direct opposition to the portrait of the elder Heyst, in which his presence is most palpable: "[Heyst] glanced at the portrait of his father, exactly above the head of the girl, and as it were ignoring her in its painted austerity of feeling" (p. 359). At the climax of the novel, indeed, when Lena prepares to do battle with Ricardo for his all-too-phallic stage knife, our interest is focused on what proves to be her final struggle with a more dangerous opponent: "She had come out after Heyst's departure, and had sat down under the portrait to wait for the return of the man of violence and death" (p. 394).

In the three nineteenth-century novels the disintegrating effect of the protagonist's self-division is held in abeyance by the temporary dominance of one of the opposed tendencies within the self and the repression of the other. The two characters with whom the protagonists are each in close relationship alternately call out one of the opposed qualities within them, and at the same time incline them to submerge the other. Thus Heathcliff elicits Cathy's tempestuousness, and she is not concerned to exhibit her refinement in relation to him; but Edgar fosters "the lady" in her, and with him she for the most part holds her wildness in check. Similarly, Maggie and Jude both try to repress their sexuality in relation to Philip and Sue respectively, and the connection with them is primarily intellectual or spiritual in nature; but in relation to Stephen and Arabella respectively this side of themselves tends to be dormant and the sexual is predominant.

In *Victory* something like the same kind of alternation is apparent when Heyst meets Lena, though the change, if not as clear cut as in the nineteenth-century novels, has perhaps greater psychological verisimilitude. The ghost of Heyst's father, in its long-accustomed presence, it appears, is not easily repressible. Before the meeting with Lena, the ghost remains in virtually unchallenged possession of Heyst, and there are no more than sporadic forays against his dominance — as in the letter writing and the conviviality with McNab previously referred to. Heyst's involvement with Morrison is a more serious manifestation of the suppressed part of himself, but though his compassion for Morrison is genuine enough, he never really commits himself to the relationship, and merely suffers stoically the consequences of the tie which he sees himself as having formed "in a moment of inadvertence" (p. 199). The dominance of the ghost, before the advent of Lena, is apparent, first in Heyst's fifteen long years of solitary wandering and then in his lone existence on the island for two years before he brings Lena to it — though it is true he is tended by Wang, another ghostly presence.

When Heyst meets Lena, his life is transformed. An immediate indication of such transformation is the impetuous way he, the detached solitary, for whom life is no more than a spectacle, forms an attachment, proceeds to act decisively on the basis of it, and then gives himself in love. If he is surprised, when he embraces Lena in the passage already quoted, by "that ready impulse towards himself which [has] been dormant in her passive attitude," it would seem that the force which impels him towards her is of a similar nature. He is certainly active enough then, and the plain facts of what follows should be sufficient to refute any suggestion that he is unable either to act or to love. It is with unaccustomed "audacity" (p. 77) that he snatches the girl from the Zangiacomo band and takes her back with him to his island; and the audacity is accompanied by a readiness to give of himself: "I am here," Lena tells him, "with no one to care if I make a hole in the water the next chance I get or not" (p. 78)—and, with his compassion aroused, Heyst shows that he is as ready to plunge after her as he was with Morrison. At this point his household ghost is held at bay, and we are told that "his sceptical mind" is now "dominated by the fullness of his heart" (p. 83).

The couple thereafter consummate their love, and once again the facts of the matter should scotch the view that Heyst is subject not only to an emotional incapacity for love but also to sexual impotence or deficiency: on the island he is said to be "under the fresh sortilege of their common life, the surprise of novelty, the flattered vanity of his possession of this woman; for a man must feel that, unless he has ceased to be masculine" (p. 201); and his feeling is matched by Lena's own sense of magical fulfillment, for she lives in "the appeased enchantment of the senses she [has] found with him, like a sort of bewitched state" (p. 303). At the same time Heyst feels that he "no longer [belongs] to himself" (p. 245), and his readiness to lose the self not unexpectedly proves (in this sexual context) to be the means of a finding of self: "The girl he had come across, of whom he had possessed himself, to whose presence he was not yet accustomed, with whom he did not yet know how to live; that human being so near and still so strange, gave him a greater sense of his own reality than he had ever known in all his life" (p. 200).

Heyst's sense of an enhancement of self, however, does not enable him to establish an equable relationship with Lena, since it is countermanded by old fears and reservations. It is on this very occasion, when he registers his gain, that he tells her that "he who forms a tie is lost." The remark is made apropos of his relationship with Morrison, but its crass insensitivity to her feeling—and to his own—in contradistinction to his habitual percipience, betrays its obsessive nature. This, we realize, is the voice of inculcated habit—is, indeed, the voice of his father who speaks through him. It is as if the old ghost rises up to challenge the old Adam which has been so bountifully released in him, and from this point on Heyst is divided between his two allegiances.

When the protagonists in the three nineteenth-century novels are pulled with equal force in opposite directions by their divided allegiances and inclinations, one of two things happens: either the pull of one force neutralizes the other and produces a state of immobility, a kind of paralysis, as it were; or the opposed pulls are so overwhelming that they result in a tearing apart of the self, in breakdown. *Wuthering Heights* is illustrative of both processes. When things reach such a pass that Edgar tells Cathy she has no alternative but to choose between him and Heathcliff, the pulls exerted by her wish to remain Mrs. Linton of Thrushcross Grange and by her profound feeling for Heathcliff are so equal in strength that she is unable to choose. When the pressure becomes intolerable, she experiences a breakdown, succumbing to a brain fever. A disintegration of self is also projected in a loss of the will to live; and though Cathy recovers from her illness and it is in childbirth that she dies, she seems after the brain fever to want to die. In *The Mill on the Floss* Maggie in the end is faced by psychological paralysis. Needing and wanting both Philip and Stephen, she is unable to choose either, and is reduced to the kind of despair that should issue only in what Philip previously refers to as a "long suicide"—though it is at this stage that the flood providentially begins and she is made to regain an earlier wholeness of being. In *Jude the Obscure* Jude's death figures a prior disintegration of self. Married once again to Arabella but still in love with Sue and longing for her, though she is married again to Phillotson, he is torn in two and deliberately courts death. He seeks, as he says, "to do for [himself]," and in effect commits suicide.

The two processes of paralysis and disintegration are also exemplified in the case of Heyst. His paralysis takes two forms. In relation to Lena, it manifests itself in his inability to say what he feels, issuing in his failure on three significant occasions to declare his love for her. On the first occasion she reproaches him, saying: "You should try to love me!":

> He made a movement of astonishment.
> "Try!" he muttered. "but it seems to me—" He broke off, saying to himself that if he loved her, he had never told her so in so many words. Simple words! They died on his lips. "What makes you say that?" he asked. . . . He did not know what to say, either from want of practice in dealing with women or simply from his innate honesty of thought. All his defences were broken now. Life had him fairly by the throat. (p. 221)

Heyst, we register, has not seemed to suffer from a "want of practice" in all the other ways in which he has "dealt" with Lena. Nor is it life which has him "by the throat," preventing speech; it is his skeptical mind, bound by the habits and beliefs of a lifetime—and bound too to a demanding ghost—that prevents him from declaring his love. We may assume he is inhibited in a similar way on the last night of Lena's life. First, as the danger posed by the predatory trio grows more palpable, Heyst ensures that Lena will not stay alone in the house when he goes to confront Jones, but when they part and she puts his hand to her lips, he can do no more than speak her name "under his breath": "He dared not trust himself—no, not even to the extent of a tender word" (p. 373). Then, even when she is dying, he cannot bring himself to tell her he loves her: "Heyst bent low over her, cursing his fastidious soul, which even at that moment kept the true cry of love from his lips in its infernal mistrust of all life" (p. 406).

In relation to Jones, Heyst's paralysis takes the form of an inability to act decisively against him. On the climactic night of confrontation he misses his opportunity when Jones, who has been covering him with a revolver, is disconcerted by the announcement that there is a woman on the island:

> Backed hard against the wall, [Jones] no longer watched Heyst. He had the air of a man who had seen an abyss yawning under his feet.
> "If I want to kill him, this is my time," thought Heyst; but he did not move. (p. 387)

Heyst's immobility here is expressive of the way in which his wish to protect Lena and safeguard their life together, which makes him perceive clearly enough that this is the moment to act against his flabbergasted opponent, is neutralized not only by a reluctance to kill but by an engrained belief in the futility of all such action. That it is not the morality of killing which is at issue is indicated when Jones marches Heyst at the point of a gun to the house in which Lena, unknown to Heyst, has received Ricardo:

In [Heyst's] breast dwelt a deep silence, the complete silence of unused faculties. At this moment, by simply shouldering Mr. Jones, he could have thrown him down and put himself, by a couple of leaps, beyond the certain aim of the revolver; but he did not even think of that. His very will seemed dead of weariness. He moved automatically, his head low, like a prisoner captured by the evil power of a masquerading skeleton out of a grave. (p. 390)

As in the case of Heyst's failure to declare his love for Lena, it is not "unused faculties" which are the problem, for he has shown that he can act decisively enough when he wants to. In this episode, moreover, in contradistinction to the scene in Jones's house, Heyst does "not even think" of taking action against his adversary, though the necessary action would mean no more than a shouldering. The paralysis of his will, which seems "dead of weariness," is attributable to the force which neutralizes his readiness to put up a fight, and indeed he is "like a prisoner captured by the evil power of a masquerading skeleton out of a grave." The simile refers directly, no doubt, to Mr. Jones, who literally has him prisoner, and who just previously is twice called a skeleton (pp. 383, 389), but it is the ghost of Heyst's father that effectively holds him back and so paralyzes him here.

The upshot of Heyst's failure to act is the death of Lena. When he first sees her with Ricardo and doubts her fidelity, he thinks that a man who has experienced "such a feeling" has "no business to live" (p. 392). We may infer that when he discovers that, far from being unfaithful, she has in effect died for him, his life is made even more intolerable. The prisoner of another ghost now, torn apart by the two spirits which contend for his soul, he takes his own life.

Robert Caserio

The Rescue and the Ring
of Meaning

The evaluative function of criticism is reluctant
to loosen its grip on the study of Conrad. Still insisting on
"sloppy" or "bad" writing at both ends of his career, on
immaturity at first and exhaustion at last, evaluation continues to control our picture of both Conrad's work and his
life. What if—for the moment—we suspend this evaluative
function? It may enable us to arrive at what judgmental
criticism has not seemed patient enough for: an adequately
appreciative description or redescription of Conrad's work,
especially in its last phase, after *Victory*. The attempt, of
course, has been made already. It has not succeeded, because
it does not come to terms with what criticism of the English
novelistic tradition often is embarrassed by—romance. *The
Rescue: A Romance of the Shallows*, my focus in this essay,
appears to have had its critical fate determined when Virginia
Woolf noted how difficult she found referring the feelings of
the novel's heroine to "the feelings of a living person" rather
than to a fantasy-romance personage. We find Woolf's discomfort repeated in the evaluative stance. Even when a critic
says he devalues late Conrad on the ground of Conrad's
failure to use language artistically, he appeals to reality, and
uses the words *romance* or *romantic* in some pejorative sense,

to confirm his analysis. Romance elements are devalued on the ground of their incompatibility with the reality and the literary realism allegedly exhibited in a superior way by Conrad's canonized work.[1]

I think we can put to rest the stubborn critical censoriousness concerning Conrad's romance. And we can do so without rejecting either romance, or realism, or truth telling. *The Rescue* in its inception belongs to the moment of *The Nigger of the "Narcissus"* and that novel's famous preface. My contention is that *The Rescue*—not overtly but implicitly—extends the preface and constitutes a dramatized *ars poetica* of the novel. It instances in narrative form the author's earliest and latest sense of the interrelations of reality, romance, and the novel; and the procrastination of *The Rescue* may be the result, below the conscious difficulty, of an unconsciously cunning delay of an *ars poetica* until the novelist had long tested—and long been tested by—his art. The result for Conrad is a justification of the romance element present in his work since *Almayer's Folly*. This justification turns on the probability I propose especially to argue: that romance is the sign of Conrad's defense of the representational nature of his novels and of their truth to the world.

To say this is to propose both a paradox of literary history and a paradoxical association of ideas. In what follows in this essay, an attempt will be made to justify both paradoxes and to exhibit an underlying logic in them; but at the start I will simply assert them and at once set out further ideas and connections that for Conrad follow in the wake of the paradoxes. The word, the form, the phenomenon of *romance* mean in Conrad things not associated with the word *romance* now, and things being driven from association with it during the time of Robert Louis Stevenson. These associations became *for Conrad* a link of romance with art's attempts at veracious representation. In Conrad's view literary representation is faithful to reality understood as one or another incontrovertible human *donnée* or given. This *given* the novelist discovers or comes upon, but does not fabricate. He then gives back to the reader this *donnée*, which is already in the reader's awareness. Such a sense of representation is imbedded in and shapes *The Rescue*, which in effect claims representation itself as a primal romance no realism can dispense with. The much-maligned love interest of *The Rescue* would not be maligned if it too were understood as the vehicle of Conrad's meditation on the novelist's romantic love of reality. The hero or heroine dramatizes the quest for something each can call real—a romance quest that for Conrad is proper to novelistic representation. But it *is* a burdensome quest. If its faithful pursuit is compromised, Conrad insists, the result is more than a fictive matter. It is a matter of life and death. In the last chapter of *The Rescue* a ring I suggest stands for Conrad's representational art is thrown away. That art is thereby called a "dead talisman," an unimportant prop on the stage of the ordinary world of normal probabilities and indeterminate appearances. Considered as this stage prop the ring is merely "romantic," a token of a fantastic and factitious realm neither real nor capable of representational truth. In Conrad's story the dead talisman spells the death of representation as a union of romance with the discovery of truth. Yet the way the ring and its romance of representation are jettisoned at the novel's end is offered us as an emblem of a hateful trivializing of the function of writing. *The Rescue* becomes a tale of the withdrawal of novelistic representation from the world—and the author asks us to feel the withdrawal as an outrage.

But we cannot feel or judge the outrage, nor understand Conrad's dramatically presented ideas about representation, without attending to his ideas about something else. The withdrawal of representation from the world as Conrad shows it is the result of modern life's having become a form of all-pervasive imperialism. Conrad sees imperialism in everything: not only in power and profit taking but in psychic and epistemological states of affairs; not only in foreign soil but in the domestic realm. And what he sees of imperialism everywhere Conrad judges to be hateful. The imperialist as Conrad portrays him reduces his opposition to what he calls primitivism. The opposition may be a foreign state; it may be also a way of knowing the world, even by way of the romance of representation. Conrad in effect says that to despise genuine romance as Conrad presents it is part of the manner of imperialism, which accepts romance in only two reduced forms: as exclusively different from reality, or as a sign of universal indeterminacy. In the canonized Conrad we may have lost direct sight of Conrad's own analytic resistance to imperialism and to imperialism's characteristic reductions, even of romance. And of course Conrad himself did not escape his own share of imperializing reductionism. In *Heart of Darkness* and *Lord Jim* the natives portrayed are reduced not by Kurtz or other whites any less than they are reduced by the author to a state we vulgarly call aboriginal. In the former work especially the virtual fetish the author makes of indeterminacy seems all too anxious a cover for the reductively determinate presentation of the Congo natives as cultural nonentities. Yet Conrad does not do this elsewhere. In *Nostromo* he presents the native culture's primitivism as a secondary product, as an advanced fabrication of imperialism. And Conrad nowhere portrays the highly civilized complexity of native cultures, and his own hostile disbelief in imperialism, as he does in the trilogy of which *The Rescue* is the last, and *Almayer's Folly* and *An Outcast of the Islands* the first two. Tom Lingard himself, the hero of *The Rescue*, and the figure on whom these overtly antiimperialist novels turn, is shown to diminish in stature as he becomes increasingly the guardian of white ego and Western conventions. His final disappearance in Europe stands for the reabsorption by the West of his adventurous youthful break with the mind and heart of imperialism.[2]

The revolt against imperialism is the sadly doomed adventure of *The Rescue*. The same revolt is also the romance of *The Rescue*. In working toward the role of novelistic representation in this adventure I must point out more fully how Conrad's treatment of native peoples in the Lingard trilogy of novels does not show them to be primitive. In this way I will be best able to point out how Conrad's fullness of treatment is inspired most of all by a specific British literary—and romance—form of antiimperialism, in a way that will help disclose the logic of the paradoxes suggested earlier. The scene of the Lingard trilogy is Malay culture. In *The Rescue*, which is set in the early 1860s, Lingard has been working for two years to reinstate Rajah Hassim and his sister Immada to the rule of the native state of Wajo. They have been exiled by "a civil war, fostered by foreign intrigues"; it appears "the Dutch want things just so."[3] Whatever the imperialist power wants, however, Lingard has helped make an alliance among the Wajo rulers and three other white-exiled or white-threatened Malay groups. This alliance is on the eve of the move to retake Wajo when a yachtful of proimperialist English arrive and are stranded on the scene. The latter are then bent on getting help from the British and Dutch authorities, and thus on calling the Western powers to the very site of the native strike force. So Lingard is faced with the job not of helping whites but of keeping the native alliance together—for its various elements fall into conflict in a self-destructive way over whether or not the strayed whites should be taken hostage. It is of course not the primitivism of the natives that is effecting the conflict here, but the diversity of their culture. And this diversity, even in its disunifying effects, Conrad equates with high civilization, with the refinement of principles governing conduct into ideologies that frame, practically and philosophically, all aspects of life.

Illustrating what is at stake in this diversity that marks civilization's refinements, one of the most important of Conrad's native characters is Tengga, the leader of one of the threatened groups. We learn he is perhaps the most controversial of the native rulers, for he is said to be selfishly opportunistic, to be "a mere shopkeeper smitten by a desire to be a chief" (p. 294). He is suspected of wanting the strike-force arsenal for profitable capital's sake, not for Wajo restoration's. Yet he is more than these accusations allow. Tengga is a more militant Muslim than Belarab, the ruler of the exiles' temporary settlement; he and his holy man "had been fighting the Dutch for years"; and Lingard's pivotal lieutenant, Jörgenson, thinks it "a pity Tengga is not chief . . . instead of Belarab." Uncertain as Tengga's character remains, however, it is indeed the special mark of Malay values that his economic motives are least trusted. Sherif Daman, another of the leaders, is in the economic scheme of things something of a pirate; and unlike Belarab and Tengga he is rashly impulsive. Yet his motives are not mercantile, and his impulsiveness is understood as the sign of generosity, so that the Wajo princess—in Lingard's absence—desires the arsenal be put in Daman's charge rather than Tengga's. The Wajo themselves are traders who subordinate mercantile exchange and profit to antiimperialist political intrigues. It is for this political reason that Conrad describes them as "romantic" (pp. 67–68). Early in the novel Conrad thus explicitly gives romance a political bearing. And, as we shall see, Conrad also uses the Wajo's romance address to economics as a model for the way he dramatizes his version of representation as a kind of gift economy. The profiteering motives the Malays suspect in Tengga are what they think of as barbarism. In contrast the piratical rover Daman (he belongs to the Malay version of the pirate brotherhood that shapes the hero of *The Rover*) is thought to be more civilized, more responsible to a citizen's virtues rather than to a capitalist's. The Malays differentiate thus between citizens and capitalists; but whatever final weight we give their internal debates, they do have significant bearings on *The Rescue*'s drama. If for the moment we put aside their relation to the economic side of Conradian representation, these debates show that, however uneasy the Malay diversity makes its components, the natives do not seek to dominate each other as the whites seek to dominate them. By contrast the whites are shown to have no respect for their own social and ethical complexity any more than for the natives'. Moreover, they seek to dominate the natives by lumping all Malay shades of ideological difference into one category: the primitive. In the fact alone that to the natives Tengga, who is perhaps most like the whites, appears to be less civilized than Daman, we can see that for European readers of the scene Malay civilization, and Lingard's alliance with it, is bound to be misread.[4]

The source of Conrad's representation of native complexity is, obviously, history itself. But *The Rescue* is not the history of the shallows, but their romance. Between imperialist history and the representational art of the novel falls this shadow, romance. Now there is a necessity in the nature of representation, as Conrad sees it, that demands a difference between *what* is represented and the representation itself. Romance is for Conrad a name for the form and nature of that inevitable difference, a difference that is — as I shall point out later — the very means by which the decided truth of an artistic representation is secured. But the form and nature of representation cannot be discussed without reference to history, both extraliterary and literary. Any misreading of the scene of *The Rescue* depends upon a missing reading. At the root of Conrad's complex picturing of native cultures is another novelist, whose name is as relevant to Conrad studies as any: Walter Scott. It was Scott who gave to Conrad, as late as 1918–19, the model of opposition to notions of the primitive. And to say that "romance is the sign of Conrad's defense of the representational nature of his novels and of their truth to the world" makes sense, and will be convincing, only in the light of Scott's inspiration. For it was also Scott's work that arguably gave Conrad the model for the interidentity of romance with the discovery of truth via novelistic representation. The traditional reading of Scott hides from us this possible way of seeing Scott's influence, because—in Scott's name—criticism opens an unbridgeable opposition between romance and reality or realism. The result is an excessive, abstract differentiation, whereby interpreters neglect a necessary dialectic of *relative* difference between what is represented and the representation itself. This dialectic is implicitly dramatized by Scott's refusal to allow romance and reality to become antitheses in his work. Scott suggests to Conrad how similarity can be found through and within dissimilitude, and the suggestion depends upon trust that this similarity is an experiential given we indeed can find.[5]

Now for all his relevance to Conrad, Scott is not much mentioned in Conrad studies.[6] Mickiewicz *is* a name joined with Conrad's; yet his poem, the Polish national epic, is also inspired by Scott's influence. And like Poland, Scotland in the eighteenth century became the extreme victim of imperialism: the Act of Union in 1707 made Scotland an English colony and reduced the Scottish to—primitives. But be these influences and parallels as they may, the great obstacle to linking Scott and Conrad remains the use of romance, whereby these novelists most essentially parallel each other. Scott passes his opposition to the idea of cultural primitivism on to Conrad in the guise of an event Scott made the es-

sence—and the essential romance element—of his own fiction: the event of the rescue. Conrad makes the romance of
the rescue in Scott into his own content and into his own
formal romance of representation. Before we can turn to the
formal aspect of Conrad's romance, I must describe the content of the rescue in Scott which inspires Conrad's later
versions of it.

Scott's novels portray the social and psychological effects
of the seventeenth-century English revolution that, long before 1789, began—for England at least—the modern world.
In the killing of the king, in the slaying of a central divine
authority, what comes to birth is the essentially decentralized
modern social order, ruled by bureaucracy. By this revolution
authority is liberated, distributed, and republicanized. Now
Scott was fascinated by the king whose central paternal authority had been broken up and redistributed by the revolution; nevertheless, Scott sided with the violence of the
youthful state that destroys authority when authority has
ceased, above all, to be generous, when authority has ceased
to give life or when it merely and possessively holds life
without sharing it. Yet in allying himself with the revolutionary, modern side of things, Scott also became the critic of
modernity. For in his novels he reveals the curious ways in
which the modern world unconsciously reproduces the pos-
sessiveness of the ancient regime and even becomes less generous than the old order. That old order had one advantage. It
embodies its tyrannies in persons, who could be swayed at
times, in the face of the pressures of flesh and blood, to be
generous. But the new order, by its depersonalizing of social
institutions, exchanges the immediate responsiveness of the
old oppressive father for an impregnable mediacy. The new
state of affairs authoritatively disclaims its authority in the
face of appeals made to it for a more giving and responsive
awareness of unsatisfied desires. Modern order and law be-

come a new imperium and a new imperialism, pervaded by what Dickens following Scott was able best to name: an order of infinite circumlocution. What was to have been redistributed has been instead postponed or deferred, and dissipated by specious exchange. The deferral of desire, the substitution of authority by the enthronement of substitutions, make modernity a network of frustrations.

Scott mostly accepted this development as the probable hazard of civilization itself, of the order of things grown complex by the transmission of liberties from kings to citizens. At the same time he uses the rescue event or action to represent a necessary recourse against the new imperialism, on the part of persons who have become victims of modern ungenerous authority. Both Edward Waverley and Colonel Talbot take this recourse on each other's behalf, and Jeanie Deans gives us an even more striking example of it when she sets free the Whistler than when she pursues legal pardon for her criminal sister. The victims of modern authority are deprived by civilization of the very life —physical or moral — civilization ought to secure them. In the face of this deprivation the victim must recapture the greater gift of life the violent revolution against kings set out originally to capture. There is thus always a moment in Scott's novels when men and women, on each other's behalf, take into their hands either the tyranny of law or the lawful tyrant, and cut the knot of oppression. They thereby rescue their own desire from suppression by an authority expressly intended to guarantee the satisfaction of desire. Violently rebellious as this lawless action is or may be seen to be, it is not primitive or even imperfectly civilized. The lawlessness is the re-presentation of the attack on authority that is the origin and guarantee of modernity's improvement on the past. The lawlessness expresses what Conrad, using Scott's rescue event, formulates more powerfully than Scott, by calling Lingard's motive for the rescue of Hassim and Immada a "tenderness that could only be satisfied by backing human beings against their own destiny" (p. 162). This tenderness, liberated by the rescue, faces a destiny that is not a heart of darkness, but the trammels of restraint civilization sets for the liberty it ought not to fail to achieve. The rescue is thus an act of civilization; the rescuer, for all his violence, is nothing less than genuinely political, a true citizen, and a truly modern one.

It remains the fate of the rescuing agent, nevertheless, in Scott and the case of Conrad's young Lingard, to be identified with what is merely primitive. Why is the genuine citizen so misrepresented in the eyes of those who oppose the rescue? As Scott presents that form of action, its violence, its lawless liberation—whether physical or spiritual—epitomizes romance. In the revolution's own extremity of license and political ardor, the revolutionary thrust against authority recaptures the romance glamor of the old order. But while the modern world, with its bureaucracy and impersonal regulation, is in fact the becalmed or arrested state of the romance of revolution, modernity grows forgetful of that fact. And once it has exchanged generous liberty for mere possessions and for selfish ambitions, the modern mind imperializes over what it has estranged from itself—the generous violence, the citizen's tenderness—modernity's foundations. Hence the modern consciousness falls. Hence it drives a wedge between its own ordinary reality and romance. It cannot see that the romance of the rescue is its own self—its exact and authoritative representation. Modernity denies the authoritative ring of meaning inherent for itself in the rescue action.

This, then, is the content and the meaning of the rescue as Conrad derives it from Scott. But in repeating and elaborating Scott in the era of Woolf, Conrad finds himself in a literary-historical dilemma. Wanting to be modern, Conrad knew the content of *The Rescue* to be as old as Scott. Perhaps Stevenson had been the last novelist before Conrad to use Scott seriously, yet when he did so in 1894 — in *Weir of Hermiston* — Stevenson set a precedent for modern criticism by using Scott to seal off romance from reality, to make romance a pure hermeticism of art. But just this insistence on artistic hermeticism may have given Conrad the challenge to spark the solution to his dilemma. He seems to have realized that Scott's content provides insight into the form of novelistic representation itself — insight to be used against Stevenson's radical aestheticizing of Scott and romance. Conrad could thereby dramatize the romance of the rescue event as a counter-Stevensonian *ars poetica*, as the story of representation in art transcending art so as to stand for life. Conrad makes even Mrs. Travers and Lingard discuss this paradoxical story. Mrs. Travers says she feels she is living with Lingard in something factitious, an opera. And this reminds Lingard of seeing an opera in Melbourne. Was the opera's story not "a defiance of all truth"? In answer Lingard says "of the few shows I have seen that one was the most real to me. More real than anything in life" (p. 301). This is Lingard's — and Conrad's — assertion in favor of representation directly, of representation's truth to life even as it differs from life. Making Scott's rescue event into his own formal romance of representation, Conrad hazards the idea that the difference between what is represented and the representation itself enables us to match different things — romance, an old story that defies truth, and life; and to find similarity given within this dissimilitude.

But where the differences between the old story — between the allegedly purely factitious thing no less than the allegedly primitive thing — and reality are stressed as a primary, forever unbridgeable distance, there can be no genuine representation for Conrad. It is worth repeating that what this means for Conrad is not only aesthetic but political loss. Through the responses of Travers to Lingard and the Malays Conrad makes this markedly clear. In the first chapter of part 5 of *The Rescue* one finds a long, masterfully nuanced argument between the stranded English yachtsman and his unhappy wife. This confrontation presents the civilized imperialist mind—Travers's—blindly castigating the romantic origins of his modernity, and calling those origins primitive. In Travers's rejection of "lawless characters, romantic personalities" (p. 270), Conrad is dramatizing Travers's distance from ultimate and essential reality. Insisting on his unqualified distance from Lingard, Travers denies the authority with which romantic personality and its actions can stand for an essential given of Travers's own identity—for the inherence of Travers's own freedom in Lingard's relative unlikeness from Travers. Travers cannot see that romance as Lingard embodies it denotes an ultimate political *reality* that can be seen *as* romance and *in* romance.

But to a Travers no representation, romantic or otherwise, could invade life with any claim of ultimate significance. If Lingard treats such an invasion into his life as an ultimate appeal especially to the tenderness of the citizen, it is because he believes in representativeness itself, in trustworthy likenesses between himself and what he stands for. But how can we think of a representational event or person or image—above all of any representation in novelistic art—as standing for anything in an authoritative, ringingly true way? Is it not possible instead—is it not probable instead—that the ring of representational meaning is the fiction rather than the truth of a moment, the arbitrary fabrication of a likeness that is the essential fiction of any moment in art? Do things stand for each other in ways—to be Travers-like and thoroughly skeptical about it—ways that are other than passing caprices of likeness? Putting aside the historical conditionings of representation in art and elsewhere, it is well to linger just here over a possible nature of representation Conrad would *not* ten-

derly back. To go further into the drama of *The Rescue*, we
need to appreciate what substitute for representation representation itself needs to be rescued from. And it is only fair to
consider, as I believe Conrad considers, how antagonism to
representation in Conrad's sense is not only the product of
stupid imperialist minds like Travers's. Imperialism, too—
yes, we must admit it—has its nobility: witness Mrs. Travers.
Because she will come to betray representation itself without
being a mere villain, it is necessary to appreciate what in one
way or another might be the position from which she helps
undo *The Rescue*'s version of romance.

It has certainly been argued by great minds, most of all in
the modern era, that representations do not have—as Conrad
in contrast claims they have—truthful or ultimate connections to what they stand for. If we represent x as y, the
argument goes, and if we say we do so because y is authoritatively like x, we are perhaps being inventive but not,
after all, truthful. For representation is arguably only an
invention of a referent, thus a fabrication rather than a revelation of what it stands for. According to this argument (again,
it is in great contrast to Conrad's assumptions) representation
is a form of the *possibility* of a thing's being—an expression
of how something *seems*, but not of how something *is*. By this
account representations arrive at no ultimate interpenetra-
tion or revelation of their referents; nor do their referents
arrive at an ultimate of expression through their representa-
tives. The definitive representation of things is always
thwarted, and the thwarting is itself the stimulus of a never-
ending dispersal and deferral in the order of representations.
Such is the view, for example, of Wallace Stevens. I cannot tell
if his mind is the reflex of an American imperialism, but it is
certainly a great mind. And when Stevens tells us that on any
ordinary evening in New Haven "reality . . . may be a shade
that traverses / A dust, a force that traverses a shade," he

makes out representation to be a forceful but fictive caprice of likenesses, a shadowy momentary traversal of shadows. In contrast Conrad sees representation as the only entry to a reality otherwise shadowed by appearances but not in itself momentary, capricious, or substanceless. This gap between two levels of the real—between what is real at the level of appearances (in their shallows, as it were) and what is real at an ultimate depth—is a gap upon which Conrad bases the nature of *his* representations. This gap between appearance and essence gives the skeptic reason to doubt representation altogether, but it gives Conrad the rescuer of representation the opportunity to match different things in a way that shows the truth of identity emerging within the appearance of difference. The revelation of a match suddenly revealed within relatively differing appearances is the gift of the shallows. According to the Conradian point of view, we can trust y's standing for x because the representation enables us to see y, albeit different from x, as an identity of x; and therefore we can see y, which is different from x, *given in x*.[7]

A passage from *The Rescue* will make this representational algebra more vivid and more clear. The Travers party, two of whom are about to become hostages, are preparing for dinner:

A pair of stewards in white jackets with brass buttons appeared on deck and began to flit about without a sound, laying the table for dinner on the flat top of the cabin skylight. The sun, drifting away toward other lands, toward other seas, toward other men; the sun, all red in a cloudless sky raked the yacht with a parting salvo of crimson rays that shattered themselves into sparks of fire upon the crystal and silver of the dinner service, put a short flame into the blades of knives and spread a rosy tint over the white of plates. A trail of purple, like a smear of blood on a blue shield, lay over the sea.

On sitting down Mr. Travers alluded in a vexed tone to the
necessity of living on preserves, all the stock of fresh provi-
sions for the passage to Batavia having been already con-
sumed. It was distinctly unpleasant.

"I don't travel for my pleasure, however," he added; "and
the belief that the sacrifice of my time and comfort will be
productive of some good to the world at large would make up
for any amount of privations." (p. 146)

Nobly intent upon his privations, Travers could never see the
sun's putting of flame and blood into the crystal and silver as
anything but a mere figure of speech. And Travers would
understand the figure to be spoken by a fabricator of rhetorical substitutions rather than by an utterer of actual and given
relations. For Travers's way of reading, that is to say, the flame
and blood provide only a possible way of representing a
passing effect of light. This possible way is a momentary
substitution for some other possible momentary way of
seeing. Presumably the representation will change with the
light brought to bear on the object; and, as the case here
suggests, from Travers's point of view that light is always
fleeting. In this fleeting light representation is seen to fabricate the substitution of one term for another, to exchange
arbitrarily one name or description for another entirely different and equally arbitrary. But for Conrad, Travers's way of
seeing is trivially beside the point. The point Conrad wants
to make in representing the silver and crystal as blood and
flame is an identification of the two in a way not arbitrary.
The figures of speech in this passage depend upon what the
novel's drama figures as a whole. And the whole drama
means to represent civilization's artifices as life-and-death
matters identical with native blood. The y term here, the
artifice of civilization, stands for blood and flame because it is
of and *in* them, is more identical with them than different

from them. So the light Conrad means to shed is not capricious and momentary, but definitive and ultimate. The match Travers would take to be arbitrary Conrad takes to be true. Although there is indeed a smear of blood over this scene, over this artifice, the "civilized" man wants to shield himself from being matched with this smear. He wants to emphasize the deferment of the match, the emphatic difference of its component terms. The "civilized" man may also claim that the shield is not his, but the primitive mind's defense against differences and differentiations that can never constitute identity but can only merely play with matches. Yet Conrad uses the drama of *The Rescue* to insist that the modern world cannot shield itself from what its shallow appearances stand for: absolute claims of blood and cries for blood that root modernity in Scott's "primitive" romance, and that double civilization in the rescue event.

In order to persuade his reader that *his* romance is not itself a capriciously fabricated likeness of reality, Conrad goes further in dramatizing representation in relation to imperialism. He also treats imperialism's economy, its habits of trade and exchange. Reading *The Rescue* we see repeatedly its economic language and motifs—the title of the last part, "The Claim of Life and the Toll of Death," is an example. Conrad connects this economic language with representation by attempting to contrast the latter with a system of exchange in which all the novel's characters—and the novelist himself—are potentially trapped. Insofar as his own novel is a product of trade, Conrad wants it to be identified with the Wajo trade, which is the political romance of rescue. He wants to liberate his version of romance—his form of representation—from trade in arbitrary substitutions. Travers would see representation as an economics of exchange arbitrarily substituting one thing for another. The substitution is dictated by the agent of exchange, by his genius or force of trading power. At

Robert Caserio

best, substitution is true to the superior force of the ex-
changer, not to what is being exchanged. A falsifying equation of identity among things is thus fabricated by the trader,
who does not care if his objects of trade are enough alike to
stand for each other. Relations of faithful likeness (even in
terms of like use-value) among the things exchanged are
condemned as "romantic," fantasy relations; the only truth is
appropriation. Like the imperialist appropriator, the Malay
Tengga is under suspicion for contempt of the Wajo effort to
make an economy of romance replace an economy of trade
based on arbitrary substitutions. If Tengga intends to capture
the guns that stand for Wajo life and liberty—for Lingard's
dedication too—Tengga means to fabricate an indeterminate
meaning for those guns, to substitute a fiction of his making
for their true meaning. He will dissociate the arsenal from the
claims of life and death it stands for. This kind of dissociation
is the essence of capitalism and of its imperialist state; here
the suspect Malay is a perfect match for Travers. Like Tengga
and Travers, Conrad suggests, a novelist too may substitute a
fiction for reality, and may make his writing a form of exchange with the reader that does not represent anything but
the writer's own fabricating power. To carry out such an
exchange the writer may colonize the world's appearances,
appropriating whatever of its aspects fit the demands of his
fabrication. Even only superficial realities—let alone any
privileged depth of reality—thus would be dispersed or made
to perish by the novelist's entrepreneurship. But how can the
novelist, Conrad wonders, avoid this kind of falsifying traversal of the world?

The answer implied in *The Rescue* is that representation
must give back or re-present to the reader what is secretly but
already given in the historical world. Representation will be
true if it uncovers what gifts and wealths of life human
fabrication has covered over, what already imminent and

valuable possession has been alienated by the substitutions of capricious exchange. In *The Rescue* the romance of representation uncovers and recovers the secret *donnée* or gift of life that is the tenderness of the citizen, and the ultimate blood expressed by the artifice of "crystal," of civilization. Compromised and dislocated in exchange, Lingard's "very desire [to restore the Wajos], unconquered, but exiled, had left the place where he could constantly hear its voice" (p. 195). In contrast the art of representation will show that the desire's exile is more appearance than truth. Romance restores the voice of the citizen to where it can be heard. When Mrs. Travers discovers in Lingard her own desire for the real life of a citizen rather than for her husband's show of civilization, she feels power at rediscovering a given of her nature, a gift she thought had been lost in an indifferent exchange of substitutes for it.[8]

But Conrad's fable is shadowed by that version of representation Conrad opposes. The novel therefore dramatizes its own conflict of interests. And the gift of the life of the citizen is dramatized above all in the ring that stands for the ultimate claims Hassim the Wajo ruler and Lingard have agreed to make on each other. The ring has been given by the Malays to Lingard, who gives back and so re-presents the gift to them. The token of allies backing each other against fate, the ring is representation, ringing true just because it is given, not made up; because it can be shared, like the life it stands for, it also, like the life it stands for, is an ultimate that cannot be substituted for anything else. Early in the novel, before the action proper starts, Hassim and Lingard have exchanged or traded their lives, have quitted their debts to each other. Exchange is behind them; what is to come will be given, not traded. Yet since the ring appears in the field of imperialist power, Conrad makes the ring hover between two states, between being an item of trade and being a gift. When Lingard gives the present of the ring back to Hassim, he tells Hassim to hold it for him, to send it only if the Wajos face death. If they send it then, Lingard will be forcibly reminded not to fail them. But what Lingard will remember and respond to is not anything exchangeable: the claim of life must be looked to, answered, not traded for.

At the novel's most crucial moment Jörgenson receives the ring from the Malays, and sends it on to Lingard via Mrs. Travers. She is the only possible bearer of the ring available at this moment. Jörgenson does not tell her that the ring stands for the Wajo claim on Lingard, and that its delivery will now mean the death of at least some of the whites, as the only possible way to proceed with the Wajo restoration. Suddenly made to bear this meaning, the ring tragically is no longer the emblem of a gift; it — and life — have been forced back into the system of arbitrary trade. When Mrs. Travers suppresses the delivery of the ring to Lingard we are certain that the gift of the citizens' tenderness, of life itself, belongs *outside* this system of exchange. Lingard's paralysis at this point must be seen partly as a dramatization of unwillingness to be forced, like the ring, into a state where lives are items of forced exchange. Mrs. Travers does make the ring a trade item: by withholding delivery of the gift she exchanges the lives of the imperialists for the lives of the natives. She knows she is doing this, but deceives herself. Her means of self-deception is to deny the representational authority of the ring, which she now pretends stands for nothing definite. Enabling her to trade in lives, this pretense makes representativeness a game, again a playing with matches rather than an earnest acceptance of a true match of identity between apparently different things. The ring here is in truth identical with particular lives, with a particular political revolution. Afraid of facing life and death or truth in a decisive moment of their appearance, Mrs. Travers insists the ring has only undecidable relations to its referent. Ironically, this insistence becomes its own form of decision, one with a deadly emphasis on the difference rather than the identity between the ring and what it means. Suppressing the ring, Mrs. Travers saves the white lives. And in response to this rescue, at the expense of native blood, Travers says, "All of this is of so little importance!" (p. 456). In turn Mrs. Travers takes the ring and says, "I am left with this thing. Absolutely unimportant. A dead talisman"—and she throws it overboard.

Outrageous as is this last reduction in *The Rescue* of the favored type of Conrad's representation, Conrad shows sympathy for Mrs. Travers. Her denial is not presented as merely weak, or as peculiarly hers. The denial is Travers's, and the intelligent Spaniard d'Alcacer's; and, most important, becomes Lingard's too. Lingard relaxes his responsiveness to the claims of Wajo. This relaxation is not the reflex of erotic dazzlement, but capitulation to an easy habit of imperialist mind. He wants to forget genuine romance is a political economy, not in the least a refuge from the pressures that threaten the tenderness of citizens. But like an author weary of giving his life to representations of life which are reduced to the trivialities of exchange, Lingard wants to rest from the rigors of standing for something. Whether in the political sphere or in the artistic, those rigors are immense, Conrad wants us to feel. But the cost of relaxation is even greater, spelling ruin for the attempt to counter destiny. Conrad mimes the loss of the ring to persuade us not to lose it.

I have said that Conrad's favored version of this miming depends upon a dialectical interplay of relatively differing things, an interplay that reveals dissimilarity to be only the shallow appearance of a deeper, decided identity. Just as the romance of the rescue matches modern reality even though it appears to be modern reality's opposite, different things, persons, and events come to stand for each other—virtually to double each other—as Conrad's novel comes to its close. In fact, the more the novel's characters consciously diverge from each other—and the ending brings with it a terrible differentiation, of whites from Malays, of Lingard from the Wajo, of Lingard from the Traverses—the more Conrad uses the novel to show the shallowness of their conscious divergence and the depth of identity underlying it. The means Conrad uses to exhibit the decided matching of different things is meant to explode into the reader's consciousness as a counter to the literal explosion that is touched off by Jörgenson and that shatters the novel's constituents. Thus at the general level of representation itself Conrad gives us a victory over the particular defeat mimed by his story. What Jörgenson disintegrates, the romance of representation reintegrates. We see the reintegration in the finale's constellation of doublings that make twins of antagonists. The white yacht's Carter, who is always at Lingard's throat, begins to see his identity *as* and *in* Lingard's; he therefore takes the place of Lingard's dull mate Shaw. Shaw moves to the yacht to replace Carter and becomes a sullen double of Travers. D'Alcacer's courtesy does stand for what Travers *means* to express; and we have already seen how Travers is blind to the way Lingard re-presents Travers with the image of Travers's own civilized identity. The more the characters differentiate themselves, in fear and distrust, the more their differentiation, intensely fabricated individually, facilitates their representation by their author and then in turn shows a unity of identity stronger than the fabricated differences. Even the enemies can be seen *as* each other and *in* each other. The novelist returns that vision of unity to the reader's consciousness of the world. At the same time he shows that the dispersals and divisions which defer that unity, divide up *its* gift and parcel it out in a system of arbitrary exchange, bring those who practice the deferral to act out living forms of suicide.

The most significant match at the novel's end shows that
Jörgenson and Mrs. Travers also stand for each other and are
both suicides—even though Mrs. Travers continues to "live."
Criticism can call Mrs. Travers's destruction of the Wajo
project a mark of Conrad's misogyny only if it ignores Conrad's representational poetics, which twin Mrs. Travers and
Jörgenson. Virtual enemies, these two exhibit the mutual
suspicion of persons who are all too alike. Jörgenson had long
ago backed a native insurgence against the Dutch. Since the
failure of that effort he has lived a death in life, a version of
Mrs. Travers's experience of the shallowness of events and the
monotony of existence with Travers. Almost unconsciously
Jörgenson has waited to be recalled to life, to something he
can feel is "real at last" (p. 132). He is a stymied adventurous
soul longing to recross the waters of oblivion into a life whose
gift, Conrad says, will be "invincible belief in the reality of
existence" (p. 116). Jörgenson's situation exactly doubles
Mrs. Travers's, for the same desire for something real at last
has drawn her to Lingard. In suppressing the ring, in effect
she murders Jörgenson, but murders the call of her own
desire as well. She makes herself the dead talisman, drowning
in the sea. Jörgenson is also a murderer and a suicide. For him
"trust in the power of life is tainted by the black scepticism of
the grave" (p. 116), and his "mistrust," "contempt," and
"scorn" for life are insisted on (pp. 443, 338, 351). When
Tengga, newly Daman's ally, comes on board the arsenal ship
with the Wajo as his hostages, Jörgenson fires the explosion
he has been rehearsing since *before* the native couple were
endangered by internecine struggles. His destructive act
fulfills Lingard's fears about him (p. 331), and fulfills Mrs.
Travers's doubts about his sanity when she sees him playing
with matches (p. 368) and preparing havoc, in a way suitable
to the skepticism of the grave. This skepticism plays with
matches in absolute contrast to the earnest way Conrad plays

with matches of a representational kind. In spite of the frustrations amidst which Jörgenson blows up the persons he was to help rescue, his action does not match—does not represent—the needs of the moment. The action capriciously fabricates hopelessness, rather than represent its given presence. As much then as his "opponent," Mrs. Travers, Jörgenson betrays representativeness. The arbitrariness of meaning assigned the ring by Mrs. Travers's grave-tainted fear and skepticism is doubled by the defeat of meaning Jörgenson's faithlessness brings upon his world.

The only person to survive being present at the explosion is Jaffir, Hassim's messenger and the ring's original bearer. He wills his survival long enough to represent to Lingard Hassim's last word. Conrad projects himself through this persistent messenger, bearing a representational function onward in spite of mistrust. The very message Jaffir bears is mistrustful: "Forget." Yet the representation of even that message reveals how the mediation of different things may reveal their underlying identity. "Forget" becomes a match with lingering and remembering. To stand faithfully even for negation becomes a victory over negation. Clearly Conrad the messenger is no mere or simple unifier. If differentiation and its systematic dispersals of identities and meanings are hazardous, he must himself engage with them. His own way of representing the world in *The Rescue* differentiates the novel from the ordinary world by posing the novel as the romance of the rescue event, handed down to him from Scott. Yet just as Conrad's characters reveal their interidentity in the course of differing with each other, so Conrad trusts his romance's difference from ordinary reality will disclose an ultimately given intermingling of the two. This ultimate gift is our helpless involvement in reality and romance at one and the same time—so that with Mrs. Travers we will say, many times and in many tones, "Is all this I have heard possible? No—

but it is true." It is a saying that well expresses how our life of the moment is for Conrad the exponent of the ultimate life or death the present truly stands for. Denying this, Conrad suggests, we will be like Mrs. Travers saying to Lingard how she is weary of his always coming to her with "those lives and those deaths in your mind" (p. 355). Here her voice expresses how tired she has grown of the rescuer and his representation by becoming a voice "emotionless, blank, unringing." In 1920 Conrad's voice, in contrast to Mrs. Travers's, was even yet not unringing.[9]

Daniel R. Schwarz

The Continuity of Conrad's Later Novels

The accepted view of Conrad's later fiction—the fiction following *Under Western Eyes* (1910)—is that it represents a radical break with Conrad's prior fiction. In recent years, Conrad's later novels—*Chance* (1912), *Victory* (1915), *The Shadow-Line* (1916), *The Arrow of Gold* (1919), *The Rescue* (1919), and *The Rover* (1923)—have been discussed as symbolic tales and allegories, as if they belonged to a different genre from his previous work. Thematically, they have been seen as symptoms of Conrad's inability to deal with love and sexuality on a mature level. Yet there is scant evidence either in the "Author's Notes" written in 1919–20, in his letters, or in his nonfiction, that in his later years Conrad thought he was writing drastically different kinds of fiction or that his values had fundamentally changed. I believe that Conrad's later writing is best understood as an evolution and development of his prior methods, themes, and values. While we should not ignore the differences between these novels and his prior work, it may be time to stress the biographical, thematic, and formal continuities with Conrad's previous work.

The later novels, like their predecessors, need to be understood as expressions of Conrad's psyche and imagination.

151

Daniel R. Schwarz

They continue to test and explore ways of feeling and ways of knowing and to reflect his quest for values and self-definition. Conrad was interested in dramatizing states of consciousness to the last, and the later Conrad novels, like his prior work, explore how men cope in an amoral cosmos more than they argue for a system of values. Conrad still shows that each person sees reality according to his own needs. For example, *Chance* depends on the elaborate presentation of multiple points of view. Conrad has the omniscient narrator of *Victory* give perspectives other than Heyst's to undermine ironically that apparently strong figure and to show the reader an alternative view of Heyst. *The Arrow of Gold* consists of an appealing but imperceptive speaker, George, and a dramatic monologue between two notes provided by an editor. Conrad's later novels continue his interest in exploring heterosexual and family ties, often in the context of futile and morally bankrupt political activity. These novels are not divorced from the social and historical context in which the characters live, and they are usually as much concerned with psychological realism and social observation as his previous work.

Conrad's letters provide evidence for the continuity of his work. For example, the following passage from a 1918 letter could have been written to Edward Garnett twenty years earlier: "That is the tragedy—the inner anguish—the bitterness of lost lives, of unsettled consciences and of spiritual perplexities. Courage, endurance, enthusiasm, the hardest idealism itself, have their limits. And beyond those limits what is there? The eternal ignorance of mankind, the fateful darkness in which only vague forms can be seen which themselves may be no more than illusions."[1] In a 1913 letter to Francis Warrington Dawson, he echoes the language of the preface to the *Nigger of the "Narcissus"* (1897) when describing the artist's lonely, agonizing struggle to create: "Suffering is as an attribute almost a condition of greatness, of devotion, of an altogether self-forgetful sacrifice to that remorseless fidelity to the truth of his own sensations at whatever cost of pain or contumely which for me is the whole Credo of the artist."[2] Conrad is still a skeptical humanist who believes that man's best hope rests in personal relationships. Conrad resented those who neglected his humanism and who implicitly accused him of "brutality" and "lack of delicacy";[3] he insisted that, as he wrote in a 1908 letter to Arthur Symons, "I have always approached my task in the spirit of love for mankind" (August 1908; *Life and Letters*, 2:73).[4] Of course, despite the considerable continuity of his career, Conrad still seeks the appropriate form and style for each subject and never ceases in his search for new subjects.

In 1910 Conrad was in his fifty-third year. He had lived and written in England for sixteen years, and was very conscious that he was aging. While he had become recognized as an important novelist, he had not achieved financial success. He was regarded as an oddity even by his admirers, an outsider who wrote in English but whose temperament and values were not quite English. His self-image oscillated between, on one hand, pride in his achievement and artistic integrity to, on the other hand, disgust with his difficulties in completing his work and despair about his severe financial problems. He suffered from lack of public recognition and was still plagued by personal and artistic self-doubt. As always, writing was extremely trying for Conrad. He feared that he would leave both *Chance* and *The Rescue* unfinished and that he would not reach the goal of twenty volumes that he set for himself.[5] His relations with Ford Madox Ford and his agent James Pinker were strained, and he was beset by anxiety, hypochondria, and gout. In this frame of mind he suffered a nervous breakdown.

In *Conrad: A Psychoanalytic Biography* (1967), Bernard Meyer has written that, after the 1910 breakdown, Conrad

Daniel R. Schwarz

"could not longer afford these introspective journeys into the self."[6] But this ignores the introspective journeys of *The Shadow-Line*, *The Arrow of Gold*, and *The Rover*. One cannot agree with Meyer that, "the doubting, troubled men, like Marlow of *Heart of Darkness*, and hapless souls Jim or Decoud, caught in a neurotic web of their own creation, gave way to simple innocent creatures who, as pawns of fate, struggle with indifferent success against external influence, external accidents, and external malevolence."[7] The later fiction, like the prior work, shows that man is ineffectual in his effort to shape permanently the larger rhythm of historical events, but is able to form personal ties and sometimes to act boldly in his own or others' interest. In *The Shadow-Line* and *The Rover*, temporary personal victories give life meaning. And the act of telling in *The Shadow-Line* and *The Arrow of Gold* is a kind of affirmation; by using assertive, energetic first person narrators to structure important aspects of his own past, Conrad becomes, as he had been in the 1898–1900 Marlow tales and in "The Secret Sharer" (1909), an active presence within his works. In the later works, passionate love and deep feeling temporarily rescue life from meaninglessness, even if they only provide fragments to shore against one's ruins.

Indeed, in the years that followed the breakdown, Conrad began to achieve financial stability and some measure of personal security. Selling manuscripts to John Quinn helped alleviate his debts. On occasion, Conrad would compromise his artistic integrity by writing potboilers for *Metropolitan Magazine*. Finally, beginning with *Chance*, his books began to sell. Gradually, he began to create a public mask. In particular, he not only was concerned with marketing his works, but with how he should appear as a literary presence. He developed a public personality for interviews and dialogues with critics, and adopted sons such as Richard Curle,

Jean-Aubry, Gide, and Warrington Dawson, all of whom propagated his reputation in the world of letters and in the market place. He became more of an urbane Englishman and cultivated a stance of moderation and worldliness. Although in his last years he was somewhat shunted aside by the surge of literary modernism, represented by the works of Joyce, Pound, Eliot, Lawrence, and Woolf, he occupied a prominent place in the world of letters until his death in 1924.

Any consideration of the later novels must take very seriously Thomas Moser's splendid *Joseph Conrad: Achievement and Decline* (1957), because Moser's arguments have shaped discussion of these novels since his book appeared. In order to clarify my own position, let me recapitulate these arguments and then briefly respond.

(1) Moser claims that "The heroes and heroines of the later Conrad are sinned against themselves unsinning."[8] On the contrary, Heyst, George, Lingard (in *The Rescue*), Réal and even Peyrol act self-righteously and arrogantly as they respond to their own motives and needs. If one must choose between sinning and sinned against (an admittedly reductive polarity), one must choose the former. In these works Conrad is more interested in the psychosexual needs of his characters, and the situations those needs create, than he is in moral categories. That he wishes us to understand that Peyrol, Lingard, Anthony (in *Chance*), and Heyst do not usually make moral decisions, but psychological decisions disguised as moral ones, establishes continuity with his prior work.

(2) According to Moser, Conrad demonstrates that "we are basically sound. When trouble comes to us, we are in no way responsible for it. The fault lies elsewhere, in other people."[9] But is this true? Lingard, Heyst, Anthony, Réal and George are shown to be people who on occasion behave illogically,

irrationally, inadequately, and ineptly; certainly their behavior does not reveal them as fundamentally sound even if, like Jim, they wish to behave correctly. But although they are not involved in situations where their conduct can be measured by rigid external standards of conduct, they must choose between basic values—such as loyalty to a comrade or lover versus loyalty to oneself. Conrad continued to be concerned with the way in which man's passions, instincts, and needs trigger behavior that has unfortunate consequences. Because Conrad is obsessed with psychosexual problems, he is more interested in particulars and *less* concerned with ideals and values than in his prior work. Yet contrary to Moser's assertion, individual guilt does not disappear. Except for *The Shadow-Line*, some of the situations involving personal relations are puzzling to Conrad, and hence his standards may be less explicit. Each novel depends on a character recognizing an ethical imperative in a difficult moral situation. Parodoxically, except for *The Shadow-Line*, the later novels are, to an extent, novels of manners, but without a *norm* of manners in which Conrad believes.

(3) Moser contends that "The perceptive hero disappears."[10] But, where *is* the perceptive hero in Conrad? As I argued in *Conrad: "Almayer's Folly" to "Under Western Eyes,"* even Marlow is quite imperceptive; in any case, in most of the later novels an omniscient narrator, a surrogate Conrad, is the perceptive figure even if he provides alternative behavioral standards to those of the major characters, standards that are not as lucid as they might be.

(4) According to Moser, "By the end of 1913, Conrad's surrender to the association between love and death is fairly complete."[11] It is true that Conrad's later protagonists face an external menace (like most of the earlier ones), and most of them (unlike the earlier novels) are in love. These facts, however, hardly establish an unnatural relationship between

love and death. While death is a frequent presence in Conrad's later plots, is the mortality rate of his major characters really any greater than in his earlier fiction? Heyst is the only central figure in the novels whose death is directly related to sexual love. The example Moser cites, Renouard in "The Planter of Malata," is depicted as a pathological personality.

(5) According to Moser, Conrad is a misogynist. While there is some truth to Moser's contention, it is an hyperbole that has become an accepted critical shibboleth. The major evidence for misogyny is the views of Marlow in *Chance*; but Marlow, although an objectification of an aspect of Conrad, is, as he had been in the previous three works in which he appears, a dramatized character. Mrs. Fyne's peculiar masculinity and lesbianism derive from her compensating for an exploitive tyrannical father; her brother, Captain Anthony, compensates in equally unusual ways, namely by his inability to respond physically to Flora's need because of over-fastidiousness and lack of self-regard. Surely, Flora's idyllic relationship with Anthony and forthcoming marriage to Powell raise questions about Moser's statement that "the later Conrad's hostility to feminine self-assertion results in the immediate destruction of his women as soon as they embark on a plan of action."[12] Arlette's initiative does not destroy her but leads to her happy marriage to Réal. And Peyrol's heroic death is not the act of a misogynist. Lena's death derives not from her failure to obey Heyst or the inadequacy of her plan, but from the failure of Heyst to respond boldly and bravely when he is threatened and, in the climactic scene, from his failure to prevent the shooting.

(6) Moser contends, "The productions of Conrad's last years [*The Arrow of Gold, The Rover*, the fragment *Suspense*, and the later half of *The Rescue*] are virtually without a redeeming feature. They reveal that Conrad has exhausted his creative energy. He has no longer anything to write about

Daniel R. Schwarz

and must rework old materials."[13] Yet Moser hereby ignores the psychological complexity of his later novels and the structural brilliance of *The Rover*.

Let me turn now to the commonly held assumption that Conrad's later fiction is different in *kind* from the prior fiction. In his important study, *Joseph Conrad's Fiction: A Study in Literary Growth* (1968), John Palmer argues that Conrad's later works should be discussed as romances with strong symbolic and allegorical components.[14]

But had Conrad sought to write allegories, we would expect a writer as self-conscious as he to comment upon that. Yet one only has to reread his letters to understand the continuity of his subjects, themes, and art. His letters and author's notes show that not only verisimilitude but also the factual origins of his work were important to him. Of *The Shadow-Line*, he wrote: "The whole thing is exact autobiography. . . . That experience is transposed into spiritual terms—in art a perfectly legitimate thing to do, as long as one preserves the exact truth enshrined therein" (February 27, 1917; *Life and Letters*, 2:182–83). And in 1917 Conrad contended that throughout his career "all my concern had been with the 'ideal' value of things, events and people" (March 8, 1917; *Life and Letters*, 2:185).

Allegory depends upon the artist's imagining a moral tale and *then* creating a story to illustrate the fable. Conrad's later novels do not dramatize an ethical system. Throughout his career, Conrad's focus is on the psychic needs, motives, and eccentricities that separate one man from another. The representative aspect of his novels derives not from the situation but from the character's archetypal aspirations. Jim wants to be a courageous hero and Razumov needs public recognition as an intellectual figure. Gould wishes to be a powerful figure who uses material wealth in the service of progress. If there is a difference in the later novels, it is that Conrad deals with obsessions and repressions that are peculiarly singular to one individual character. Because Heyst, George, Anthony, Lingard, and Peyrol have their own unique psyches, they may be at times less representative of moral and cultural issues than Conrad's prior protagonists. Because his later protagonists have motives with which most readers identify, we are drawn to them; because their unacknowledged needs and obsessions are often eccentric (although eccentric in a way that to our discomfort suggests *our* repressed selves), we draw away to a distance that approximates the stance of the omniscient narrator, with whose emotional and moral standards of behavior we as readers are more comfortable.

I would like to propose an alternative view of Conrad's later novels, a view that, while acknowledging differences in emphasis from the earlier work, stresses continuities. We can divide Conrad's career after 1910 into three distinct phases. In the first, comprising *Chance* and *Victory*, Conrad wanted to demonstrate that he was an English novelist, not a Slav writing in English, as some reviewers implied. He had to prove to his audience and perhaps to himself that he had become an English writer. *Chance* and *Victory* represent Conrad's attempts to write English novels of manners and to explore the intricacies of personal relationships in the context of contemporary customs and values. He regarded *Victory* as a "strictly proper" work "meant for cultured people,"[15] and he thought that "The Secret Sharer" was English "in moral atmosphere, feeling and even in detail."[16]

In *Chance* and *Victory*, Conrad's subject matter is less his own life than the external world. But the second phase of Conrad's later novels, comprising *The Shadow-Line*, *The*

Arrow of Gold, and *The Rescue,* derives more from a personal impulse. In these works, unlike the Marlow tales, Conrad recreates emotions of the past more than he objectifies his present inner turmoil. As Conrad aged, he sought subjects in his personal and literary past, and his fiction less frequently addresses his immediate personal problems or current public issues. *The Shadow-Line* and *The Arrow of Gold* reach back into his personal past, while *The Rescue* is completed primarily to settle his longstanding personal anxiety about a work that had been stalled for two decades. *The Shadow-Line* is a fictional memoir of his initiation into command, while *The Arrow of Gold* is a fictional version of initiation into sexual maturity. *The Rescue* is a nostalgic look at both his personal past and his literary past. These worlds provide something of an escape from Conrad's present anxieties and harsher memories. *The Rescue* enabled him to recapture the romance world of Malay and of his literary youth—the period of *Almayer's Folly* and *An Outcast of the Islands,* and his favorite work, *The Nigger of the "Narcissus."* In all three works he is, like Marlow in "Youth," placing his back to the future and looking longingly into the past with the hope of recapturing past feelings of energy, vitality, and success.

In the final phase, he looks back (in *The Rover* and the incomplete *Suspense*) to the Napoleonic period and creates large historical canvases that recall his great political novels. While we do not know what he would have done in *Suspense,* his real concern in *The Rover* is coming to terms with his own approaching death. In *The Rover,* the Napoleonic era provides the occasion for a moving lyrical novel about the possibility of facing death heroically. The major character, an aging seaman and an outsider, is a fictional counterpart of Conrad.

Continuing a trend begun in the novels about politics (*Nostromo, The Secret Agent,* and *Under Western Eyes*),

Conrad's post-1910 novels are concerned with family and personal relationships, with how and why people love one another. They address how historical and social forces limit and define the possibilities for love and action. Conrad never put behind him the conviction that man was caught in a web of circumstances beyond his control. But he also believes in man's capacity to grow, to love, and to know himself. Conrad contends that within an indifferent if not hostile universe, man's indomitable will enables him to survive despite setbacks and individual failures. Thus, he is not the nihilist and the prophet of darkness that he has been depicted as in much recent criticism.

Except for *The Shadow-Line*, Conrad's later novels usually have three not completely integrated organizing principles: (1) a basic adventure tale, often a voyage, dominated by a self-sufficient, independent, one-minded male figure; (2) the heterosexual interaction between the protagonist and the woman whom he loves; and (3) the historical and social setting in which the events take place. These structural principles often stand in an uneasy relationship, particularly in the novels' second halves, where the love relationships intensify and often overwhelm the potential moral consequences of the males' behavior in the adventure. In *Chance*, for example, from the time Flora and Captain Anthony elope, the structure revolves around their relationship and undermines the baroque narrative technique. Conrad's fundamental interest in the characters' psychosexuality reasserts itself in spite of the intervention of Marlow and the nameless narrator. In fact, Powell, the nominal source of the last phase, is subsumed into the love motif because of his passion for Flora. Again in *Victory*, the external views of Heyst and the double narrator—Davidson and his anonymous listener—become less important after the elopement; the novel becomes concerned with the lovers' interaction. In *The Rover*, Peyrol undertakes his final mission less from commitment to a political cause than out of his affection for Arlette and his inability to face defeat for her hand.

In these novels Conrad's conception of heterosexual love is often bourgeois and conventionally Edwardian, but wasn't this the case in his earlier work? Moments of passion and displays of physical affection are still often depicted as extraordinary events that violate society's taboos. Conrad is ambivalent to those whose love takes place in remote settings and unusual situations and whose love thus challenges the validity of traditional manners and mores. We see a typical moment in *The Rover* when Réal suddenly kisses Arlette's hand and fastidiously interprets the kiss as a violation of not only decorum but morality. He excoriates himself for the kiss; a man of "pedantic conscience," Réal thinks of that kiss as if it had been a rape. That in *The Arrow of Gold* so much is made of Rita's reputation and her illicit relationship with Henry Allegre, and that Jóse Ortega and then Blunt become her nemesis as if in response to her passion for George, testify to the fastidious conscience of the author. The editor's patronizing view of George indicates Conrad's desire to separate himself from a protagonist who is a version of his passionate, impulsive younger self. At times the reader feels Conrad's longing for absolute standards with which to judge the passions that constitute the major subject of his later work.

To sustain my argument about the continuity of Conrad's career, I propose to return to 1910 and to look briefly at *Chance*. Conrad had the kind of writing block when working upon *Chance* that he had had several times earlier in his career, most notably while working on *The Rescue* in 1896–97. Not only did he have the severe breakdown in 1910 and a relapse in early 1911, but he also suffered several episodes of hypochondria, before completing *Chance* in 1912. As he had done when faced with writer's block before writing *The Nigger of the "Narcissus,"* Conrad used the process of beginning a voyage as a means of beginning a novel. Starting with *The Nigger of the "Narcissus,"* Conrad often used the voyage with its movement from beginning to end, its defined cast of characters, and, for him, its memories of successful action as a means of ordering his own writing process. Imagining the completion of a quest or a voyage released Conrad from the agonies of writing. As with *The Nigger of the "Narcissus,"* he thinks of *Chance* as a voyage to be completed, and writes of "having got a slant of fair wind with *Chance*" (May 1911; *Life and Letters*, 2:128). Again he relies upon his sea experience to overcome self-doubt as an author.

As he had in 1898–1900, Conrad uses Marlow when he has difficulty writing because he can transfer the problems of writing and understanding to an alter ego within the world he is trying to create. Like his creator, Marlow has retired from the sea but sustains himself with the possibility—surely a fiction in Conrad's case—that he might somehow return to that life. The subject matter of *Chance* becomes a means for Conrad's imaginatively escaping the disappointments of land and the difficulties of writing. Conrad has Marlow consistently allude to a land-sea dichotomy in reductive terms. Criticism of the land is an aggressive, if childish, response to the source of Conrad's frustrations with his personal and professional life.

Chance, the first novel after the three major political novels, sustains and intensifies the stress on private life and passionate love as the only alternatives to a world threatened by materialism, political ideology, and uncontrollable historical forces. In *Chance*, as in earlier Conrad, each man is lonely, isolated, and separate, and requires the recognition of another as friend, lover, parent, child, or counselor to complete him. This kind of recognition in the form of empathy and understanding revitalizes the recipient.

If there is an alternative to repression, isolation, and self-imprisonment in *Chance*, it is in the possibility of friendship and, most significantly, passionate love. The novel proposes the alternative achieved by Flora and Anthony and endorsed by Marlow when he arranges the union between Powell and Flora. Yet the ending should not betray us into believing that Conrad the optimist has triumphed over Conrad the skeptic or that Conrad's basic perception of man's place in the cosmos has fundamentally changed. Does marriage really ease the pain of living in a purposeless universe, in a world of meanness and pettiness? Once one perceives the prominence of the prison metaphor within the texture of the novel, one realizes that Conrad's indictment of English life has the harshness and bitterness of *The Secret Agent*. *Chance* discovers a heart of darkness beneath the civilized exteriors of Edwardian London, just as *The Secret Agent* discovers it in the political machinations not only of anarchists and reactionaries but of those charged with upholding the status quo. In *Chance*, the London of *The Secret Agent* still exists in all its shabby, ugly decadence: mankind is separated by individual dreams and illusions.

Let us turn to *The Rover*, the final novel Conrad completed, to pursue my argument for continuity. Throughout Conrad's career, he spoke of the search for solidarity with his kind and made clear that he did not want to write for a coterie. *The Rover* was written with the idea of reaching that part of the mass of mankind which was literate. In important respects, it is a synopsis of a number of major themes in his previous work. Peyrol, the rover, is an heroic version of the kind of man Conrad sought to reach. Every aspect of the novel—the style, voice, and structure—reflects his attempt to reach beyond a limited audience to those who would recognize a kinship with a forceful, competent, shrewd, but not intellectual hero. Conrad's technique is appropriate for the barely verbal and unself-conscious characters of *The Rover*. That is why the voice sometimes seems to be an articulate version of Peyrol; why the style deliberately eschews the elaborate syntax of Marlow's meditative, introspective style or the hyperbole and imprecision of such later works as *The Arrow of Gold* and the short story, "The Planter of Malata"; and why the structure avoids disrupted chronology and elaborate narrative technique. *The Rover* is a spare, bold, minor masterpiece even if it does not integrate plot, character, and historical context with the subtlety and intensity of *The Secret Agent* and *Heart of Darkness*. In *The Rover*, as in *Chance*, the small number of individuals in an isolated setting enables Conrad to insulate the characters from outside factors and to limit tangential interactions. In this way, the novel's fictional materials resemble the voyage experience with which as an artist he felt most comfortable.

For Conrad, life at sea was romance and epic, and the successful completion of a voyage such as Peyrol's climactic one is equivalent to discovering or regaining identity. *The Rover* is not only a version of the Ulysses myth, but a fictional version of *A Personal Record*; with its elegiac tone, its sense of forthcoming death, and its emphasis on returning home to discover the self that has been created abroad, Conrad's autobiographical volume anticipates major concerns of *The Rover*. *The Rover* is Conrad's *Death in Venice*. Every element combines to provide the orchestration for Peyrol's death. As in *Death in Venice*, the narrator's distance from his protagonist fluctuates; as in Mann's novella, an author is partly objectified in a character. Peyrol is the inarticulate, courageous man of action that Conrad might have become. Motivated not by commitment to political dogma but by love of country, he is the man who finally makes a difference in the affairs of his nation. *The Rover* is about coming to terms with age and dying. Peyrol fulfills Conrad's fantasy of an elegant death in a heroic action.

Conrad spoke of *The Rover* in terms that suggested its special importance to him: "I have wanted for a long time to do a seaman's 'return' (before my own departure)" (February 22, 1924; *Life and Letters*, 2:339). Peyrol's desire in his final voyage to merge his destiny with that of his nation may reflect Conrad's desire as he approached death to contribute meaningfully to Poland's destiny. His fantasy of a significant political act is embodied in Peyrol. If, like Nabokov, Conrad's life was embodied in his imagination, he was nevertheless uncomfortable that he had turned his back on politics and the heritage of his father, whom he recalled as an idealistic patriot. The novel's title also refers to himself, the twice-transplanted alien who finally found a home in England and no longer felt himself quite so much of an outsider. Peyrol recreates himself at fifty-eight when circumstances connive with his own weariness to deprive him of his past; he creates a new identity just as surely as a younger Conrad did when he left Poland to go to sea and, later, when he turned from the sea to a writing career.

The Rover combines Conrad's fantasy of retreat with his lifelong fantasy of an heroic return home. (Neither his first visit to Poland in 1890 nor his second at the outbreak of the war quite fulfilled this fantasy.) *The Rover* associates Peyrol's return with Conrad's own romantic desire to return to his past. In *A Personal Record*, writing of his first return to Poland, Conrad wrote how the faces "were as familiar to me as though I had known them all from childhood, and my childhood were a matter of the day before yesterday" (p. 27).[17]

Upon arriving in France, Peyrol is struck by the parallel between himself and the people he encounters, including even the cripple. Gradually, he feels that he belongs to France, represented in his mind by the tiny coastal hamlet in which he lies and by the people he knows there.

Peyrol is the obverse of Conrad's meditative, introspective aspect, the aspect dramatized by Marlow. Rather he represents Conrad the man of action, the man who, even while mistrusting democracy, sought solidarity with the rest of mankind. Peyrol is also a surrogate for the aging Conrad. He retires after success as a man of action and regrets the life he has left behind. He has difficulty finding a comfortable niche in his new life and, like Conrad, sustains himself with the dream of resuming his sea life. Despite formal omniscience, the distance between Conrad and Peyrol often dissolves because Peyrol is the fictional counterpart for Conrad's fantasies of a significant death to climax an heroic old age. Conrad's sympathies move back and forth from narrator to character, from his observer to his subject. Conrad's analysis of Peyrol often oversimplifies his behavior to the point of distorting it; that is, his comments do not do justice to the subtlety of his character. In a sense, Conrad is trying to write an adventure story in the Kipling and Stevenson tradition, but in the final scene his moral imagination resists the necessary structural simplicity, partly because he cannot fully separate himself from his protagonist. Peyrol need not have committed suicide to be captured; by having Peyrol take not only Scevola but also Michel to their deaths, Conrad shows once again the ambiguity of decisive action.

Since Conrad would have expected us to remember that France lost the Napoleonic Wars, Peyrol's efficacy must be measured in other than political or military results.[18] Arlette's and Réal's happy marriage derives from Peyrol's generosity. The fantasy of quiet retreat from responsibility fulfills Con-

Daniel R. Schwarz

rad's own dreams. Both Peyrol and Réal wish to escape the mesh of public events. As in *Nostromo, The Secret Agent*, and *Under Western Eyes*, political partisanship is the enemy of human relationships; even Peyrol's zealous suicidal act illustrates this. Yet Peyrol's sacrifice for Réal is Conrad's final version of the recurring moral dilemma that a man faces when he must choose either self-interest or self-abnegation. By his heroic act, Peyrol shows the meaning of fraternity as self-sacrifice with a purity and clarity that few Conradian deeds permit.

I should like to conclude with a brief evaluation of Conrad's work after 1908. "The Secret Sharer," written immediately before *Under Western Eyes*, and *The Shadow-Line* rank with Conrad's masterpieces—*Nostromo, Heart of Darkness, Lord Jim*, and *The Secret Agent*. Not so incidentally, in both works, Conrad uses his characteristic technique of a meditative mind probing the significance of a crucial past experience. While *Victory* and *The Rover* are quite splendid, even they share four flaws that occasionally disrupt the later fiction. (1) Often Conrad does not give himself as completely to the narrative voice or to his other major characters; at times, his withholding of the full range of his psychic involvement is responsible for a more flaccid form. (2) As Conrad sought a larger audience, he began to use a more conventional chronology and abandoned the nonchronological movement that depended upon the striking juxtaposition of incidents. In the work before *Chance*, Conrad's unique juxtaposition of events had enabled him to present the reader with a complex moral context for judging the actions of central characters. (3) His later novels focus on fewer characters and fewer dramatic situations and lack the moral density of the prior works. (4) He did not always successfully integrate his protagonist's private life into the historical or social background. In its way, *The Rover* addresses the French Revolution, as *Heart of Darkness* addresses imperialism, but its characters do not typify or epitomize their historical moment. *Nostromo* and *Heart of Darkness* penetrate to our deepest levels because they are representative of their *Zeitgeist* in the same way that Odysseus's journey is. What make Conrad's major novels so compelling are the tensions between public issues and private lives and between representative aspirations and idiosyncratic characters, and these tensions are often missing in the later works.

Conrad's later work contains qualities that typify the work of many older artists: the revival of forms and themes of past artistic successes, references to earlier works, nostalgia for an earlier period of life, emphases on turning points in life, and intermittent sensuality. But what is usually lacking in Conrad's later work is the creative rage of the older Yeats, the willingness to take the chances taken by the aging Monet, the bold disregard for precedents of the Joyce who wrote *Finnegans Wake*, and the Olympian turning away from mere nominalistic details to focus on essential truths that characterizes the later work of Matisse.

Notes

Conrad in the Eighties

Ross C Murfin

1. J. Hillis Miller, *Poets of Reality: Six Twentieth-Century Writers* (Cambridge, Mass.: Harvard University Press, Belknap Press, 1966), pp. 5–7.

Heart of Darkness Revisited

J. Hillis Miller

1. Karl Marx, "Manifesto of the Communist Party," in *The Marx-Engels Reader*, 2d ed., ed. Robert C. Tucker (New York: W. W. Norton, 1978), p. 476.

2. Joseph Conrad, *Heart of Darkness*, ed. Robert Kimbrough (New York: W. W. Norton, 1963), p. 7. Further references will be indicated by page numbers from this edition, which includes variants from the manuscript.

3. See Jacques Derrida, "D'un ton apocalyptique adopté naguère en philosophie," in *Les Fins de l'homme*, ed. Philippe Lacoue-Labarthe and Jean-Luc Nancy (Paris: Flammarion, 1981), pp. 445–79, especially pp. 468ff. The essay has recently been translated by John P. Learey, Jr., and published in the 1982 number of *Semeia* (pp. 62–97).

Notes

Conrad's Impressionism and Watt's "Delayed Decoding"

Bruce Johnson

1. See Ian Watt, *Conrad in the Nineteenth Century* (Berkeley and Los Angeles: University of California Press, 1979), pp. 169–80. Watt too sees the origin of the word in the context of Locke and Hume (cf. p. 171) but would probably not agree that the Lockean sense persists and helps to place Conrad in the mainstream of historic impressionism.

2. E. H. Gombrich, *Art and Illusion: A Study in the Psychology of Pictorial Representation* (Princeton, N.J.: Princeton University Press, 1969), pp. 81–82.

3. See Watt, *Conrad in the Nineteenth Century*, pp. 175–79.

4. A word of caution: the high road to understanding *Logische Untersuchungen* consists of turning immediately to part 2, "The Fundamental Phenomenological Outlook," in *Ideen*, published first in 1913. The full strategic objectives of the earlier work are nearly impossible to see without this later "introduction." See Edmund Husserl, *Ideas: General Introduction to Pure Phenomenology*, trans. W. R. Boyce Gibson (New York: Macmillan, Collier Books, 1962).

5. Jules Laforgue, "Impressionism," in "Impressionism: The Eye and the Poet," trans. William Jay Smith, *Art News* 55 (1956): 43–45. Reprinted in Linda Nochlin, *Impressionism and Post-Impressionism, 1874–1904: Sources and Documents* (Englewood Cliffs, N.J.: Prentice-Hall, 1966), pp. 14–20; these quotations pp. 16 and 17.

6. William Barrett, *Time of Need: Forms of Imagination in the Twentieth Century* (New York: Harper and Row, 1973), pp. 64–83.

7. See Avrom Fleishman's prescient application of Charles Peirce to some of Conrad's effects in *The Secret Agent*, "The Criticism of Quality: Notes for a Theory of Style," *University Review* 33 (1966): 3–10.

8. Barrett, *Time of Need*, pp. 72–74.
9. Bruce Johnson, "Joseph Conrad and Crane's *Red Badge of Courage*," *Papers of the Michigan Academy of Science, Arts, and Letters* 48 (1963): 649–55.
10. William W. Bonney, *Thorns and Arabesques: Contexts for Conrad's Fiction* (Baltimore: Johns Hopkins University Press, 1980), pp. 51–149.
11. Lilla Cabot Perry, "Reminiscences of Claude Monet from 1889 to 1909," *American Magazine of Art* 18 (1927): 119–25. Reprinted in Nochlin, *Impressionism and Post-Impressionism*, pp. 35–36; this quotation p. 35.
12. See Don Ihde, *Experimental Phenomenology* (New York: G. P. Putnam's Sons, 1979), p. 36 and, indeed, all of chapter 2.
13. Barrett, *Time of Need*, pp. 77, 79.

Conrad and the Psychology of Colonialism

Hunt Hawkins

1. John E. Saveson's *Joseph Conrad: The Making of a Moralist* (Amsterdam: Rodopi, NV, 1972) studies the contemporary influences on Conrad.
2. O. Mannoni, *Prospero and Caliban: The Psychology of Colonialization*, trans. Pamela Powesland (New York: Frederick A. Praeger, 1956), p. 108. Subsequent citations in text.
3. Joseph Conrad, "Youth," published with "Heart of Darkness" in *Youth and Two Other Stories* in the Kent edition of *The Complete Works of Joseph Conrad* (Garden City, N.Y.: Doubleday, Page, 1924–26), 16:41–42. Subsequent citations in text, by page number alone.
4. Hannah Arendt, *The Origins of Totalitarianism* (New York: Harcourt, Brace, 1951), p. 189.
5. R. A. Goonetilleke, *Developing Countries in British Fiction* (Totowa, N.J.: Rowman and Littlefield, 1977), p. 92.
6. Ezekiel Mphahlele, *The African Image* (London: Faber and Faber, 1962), p. 101.

Notes

7. Peter Abrahams, "The Blacks," in *An African Treasury*, ed. Langston Hughes (New York: Pyramid Publications, 1960), p. 60.

8. Frantz Fanon, *Black Skin, White Masks*, trans. Charles L. Markmann (New York: Grove Press, 1967), p. 94.

9. The most severe tempering of his optimism about native rebellions would come some years later in the much more complicated political situation of *Nostromo* (1904).

The Landscape of Hysteria in *The Secret Agent*

Avrom Fleishman

1. D. M. Thomas, *The White Hotel* (New York: Viking Press, 1981), p. vii.

2. David R. Weimer, *The City as Metaphor* (New York: Random House, 1966), pp. 60–61. Subsequent quotation from p. 63.

3. Charles C. Walcutt, *American Literary Naturalism: A Divided Stream* (Minneapolis: University of Minnesota Press, 1956), p. 69. Subsequent quotation from p. 67.

4. Weimer, *City as Metaphor*, p. 60.

5. *The Works of Stephen Crane*, ed. Fredson Bowers (Charlottesville: University Press of Virginia, 1969–), 1:120.

6. Thomas, *White Hotel*, p. 130. Subsequent citations in text.

7. I quote the Kent edition of *The Complete Works of Joseph Conrad* (Garden City, N.Y.: Doubleday, Page, 1924–26), 13:11. Subsequent citations in text, by page number alone.

Victory and Patterns of Self-Division

H. M. Daleski

1. Joseph Conrad, *Victory*. I quote the Dent Collected Edition (London: Dent, 1948), p. x. Subsequent citations in text.

2. Douglas B. Park, "Conrad's *Victory*: The Anatomy of a Pose," *Nineteenth-Century Fiction* 31 (1976): 153, 157.

3. Sharon Kaehele and Howard German, "Conrad's *Victory*: A Reassessment," *Modern Fiction Studies* 10 (1964): 61.

4. Douglas Hewitt, *Conrad: A Reassessment* (1956; London: Bowes and Bowes, 1969), p. 104.

5. C. B. Cox, *Joseph Conrad: The Modern Imagination* (London: Dent, 1974), p. 129.

6. Adam Gillon, "Conrad's *Victory* and Nabokov's *Lolita*: Imitations of Imitations," *Conradiana* 12 (1980): 58.

7. Donald A. Dike, "The Tempest of Axel Heyst," *Nineteenth-Century Fiction* 17 (1962): 103.

8. Frederick R. Karl, *A Reader's Guide to Joseph Conrad* (New York: Noonday Press, 1960), p. 260.

9. Albert J. Guerard, *Conrad the Novelist* (Cambridge, Mass.: Harvard University Press, 1958), p. 273.

10. Suresh Raval seems at first to take a similar view: "The very crux of the narrative turns upon the conflict generated by Heyst's divided loyalties. He is a man torn between, on the one hand, allegiance to the self of universal detachment implanted in him by his father, and on the other hand his spontaneous adherence to the call of the human community as it is embodied in Lena and Morrison." But that Raval in fact tends to see one of these tendencies as more genuine than the other is suggested by subsequent statements: "Heyst's rescues of Morrison and Lena occur in [a] context of skeptical detachment contaminated only by a pity that does not engage a deeper commitment to life"; "For Heyst, love, being grounded in reciprocal relationship, is impossible because his skeptical conception of life cannot liberate a response antithetical to itself"; "Lena seems to recognize . . . that Heyst . . . cannot possibly feel or experience love." See "Conrad's *Victory*: Skepticism and Experience," *Nineteenth-Century Fiction* 34 (1980): 420, 421, 424, 427.

11. I have traced these patterns in *Wuthering Heights* and *The Mill on the Floss* in detail in *The Divided Heroine: A Recurrent Pattern in Six English Novels* (New York: Holmes and Meier, 1983).

Notes

The Rescue and the Ring of Meaning

Robert Caserio

1. For Virginia Woolf's unsigned *Times Literary Supplement* review see *Conrad: The Critical Heritage*, ed. Norman Sherry, (London and Boston: Routledge and Kegan Paul, 1973). The finest intelligence brought to bear on a negative evaluation of Conrad's late works is Eloise Knapp Hay, *The Political Novels of Joseph Conrad* (Chicago: University of Chicago Press, 1963). Her chapter on *The Rescue* is required reading. The most recent attempt at a full-scale, intensive redescription of all late Conrad is Gary Geddes, *Conrad's Later Novels* (Montreal: McGill–Queens University Press, 1980). Geddes's readings are sensitive, but not as strong as one might wish, so that the major attempt to suspend received evaluation and to reinterpret is still John A. Palmer, *Joseph Conrad's Fiction: A Study in Literary Growth* (Ithaca, N.Y.: Cornell University Press, 1968). But—oddly enough for his project—Palmer thinks Conrad's "line of growth . . . comes to an end with *Victory*, and the works that follow are largely anticlimactic" (p. xiii). So he does not treat *The Rescue*. And while Palmer writes intelligently about Conrad's symbolism and allegory, and while he admirably attempts to justify the mixture of symbolism, allegory, and realism in *Victory*, he believes the two former elements are at odds with the latter. In this light, perhaps not surprisingly, he avoids discussion of Conradian romance except as a form of Conrad's irony. This avoidance appears to be redressed in David Thorburn, *Conrad's Romanticism* (New Haven, Conn.: Yale University Press, 1974). Yet we find evaluation also in command of Thorburn, with some baffling results. Discriminating romantic*ism* ("the specially Romantic virtue of sincerity, of truth-telling") from romance, Thorburn calls the latter "a pressing active *threat* to the seriousness and integrity of [Conrad's] work . . . his fiction is imperilled by its subject matter" (p. 13). To *The Rescue* he applies the following tags: "disappointing," "offensive," "excessive," "unconvincing," "disastrous," "sorry." In Fredric Jameson, *The Politi-*

cal Unconscious (Ithaca, N.Y.: Cornell University Press, 1981), chapter 5, on Conrad, is called "Romance and Reification." In this chapter Jameson identifies romance with mass-culture adventure tales, but the term then drops out of sight. Thus, in spite of Jameson's treatment of romance in his chapter 2 ("Magical Narratives"), I find it difficult to see or say just what romance means for Jameson's version of Conrad. Presumably the presence of romance in Conrad is one of the factors that make Jameson call him "so archaic, so regressive and old-fashioned, as to be at one and the same time post-modern, and more modern than any of his contemporaries" (p. 219). I like the literary history suggested by this sentence. Another recent view of romance, Patricia A. Parker, *Inescapable Romance* (Princeton, N.J.: Princeton University Press, 1979), emphasizes romance — especially in the modern era — as "the prospect of a perpetual regression" entailing "the impossibility of any final unveiling" of the objects of the romance quest (p. 221). The growing influence of such a view makes all the more necessary a recovery of a tradition of alternative intentions in romance. As will be seen below, Conrad would consider "the impossibility of any final unveiling" a negation of romance.

2. Decided critical recognition of Conrad's antiimperialism seems to begin with Hay, *Political Novels of Conrad*, and with Avrom Fleishman, *Conrad's Politics* (Baltimore: Johns Hopkins University Press, 1967), especially his chapter 4, "Colonists and Conquerors." Fleishman assigns the foundation of Conrad's stance to Conrad's place in the tradition of Burke's organicist philosophy of community. My essay develops a qualification of this view; see also note 6 below. For a more skeptical view of Conradian imperialism than Hay's, Fleishman's, or mine, see Robert E. Lee, *Conrad's Colonialism* (The Hague: Mouton, 1969). Recent studies reemphasizing Hay and Fleishman are John A. McClure, *Kipling and Conrad: The Colonial Fiction* (Cambridge, Mass.: Harvard University Press, 1981) and Hunt Hawkins, "The Issue of Racism in *Heart of Darkness*," *Conradiana* 14 (1982): 163–71. Hawkins suggests Conrad's opposition to racism "is perhaps clearest in his Malayan novels" (p. 169). All this criticism tends to treat the content of Conrad's anti- or proimperialism without examining

Notes

the relation of his stance to his style or his ideas about representation. In Jameson's chapter on Conrad there is scarcely explicit mention of imperialism; but an equation is suggested between Conrad's style and form and a complex imperializing bent, since this style is said to express history by suppressing history. An equally "radical" critical point of view, but with an emphasis contrary to Jameson's, is Jacques Darras, *Joseph Conrad and the West: Signs of Empire* (London: Macmillan, 1982). Darras stresses "the generative power of absolute negativity in Conrad's writing: (pp. 143–44) which overtly (and not via suppression) reveals "how empty and inadequate is the language of the West" (p. 96); that is, how language itself is an empty sign of empire. Darras curiously remains within the received evaluations: he emphasizes *Heart of Darkness* and does not treat the Malay novels. My argument about *The Rescue* claims—in contrast to Jameson and Darras—the compatibility of a rejection of imperialism with ideology-transcending representational "signs."

3. *The Uniform Edition of the Works of Joseph Conrad* (London: J. M. Dent, 1924), 11: 82, 101. Hereafter citations of this edition appear in parentheses in the text.

4. The native conflicts are given concentrated description in pp. 171–77 of *The Rescue*. Tengga has been deposed by the Dutch; his sentiments about white hypocrisy ("We must not touch . . . skin . . . like yours . . . , but at the bidding of you whites we may go and fight with people of our own skin and our own faith") repeat Babalatchi's in *An Outcast of the Islands*. Daman's characterization of Tengga ("a mere shopkeeper") has special authority because of its placement late in the drama at pp. 294–97. But even at the end Tengga stands beyond belittlement, since even the suspicious Jörgenson "had not the slightest doubt" that "Tengga was much more ready to negotiate than to fight" (p. 389). This judgment, as we shall see, places responsibility for the novel's final disaster squarely on Jörgenson as well as on Lingard. The native leader most interestingly and fully rendered by Conrad is Belarab. Increasingly pacifistic and uxorious, by the novel's end he doubles Lingard's war-delaying attachment to Mrs. Travers.

In estimating Conrad's dramatization of the Malays, Norman

Sherry's magisterial *Conrad's Eastern World* (Cambridge: Cambridge University Press, 1966) can scarcely go unnoticed. Sherry emphasizes the second-hand and bookish sources of Conrad's "knowledge" of these peoples. But whatever its sources in "dull, wise books," this knowledge is made imaginative and dramatic by Conrad, in a way the investigation of sources must not minimize or ignore.

5. This point will be developed later. For the way difference from the represented object enters into representation I draw especially on Geörgy Lukács, *Werke* (Neuwied am Rhein: Luchterhand, 1962–81), vols. 11 and 12, *Die Eigenart des Ästhetischen*; and on Richard Wollheim, *Art and Its Objects*, 2d ed. (Cambridge, Mass.: Harvard University Press, 1980), especially on Supplementary Essay 5 ("Seeing-as, seeing-in, and pictorial representation"); and *On Art and the Mind* (Cambridge, Mass.: Harvard University Press, 1974), especially on "On Drawing an Object" and on the essays about E. H. Gombrich and Nelson Goodman.

In the criticism of Scott, from Alexander Welsh, *The Hero of the Waverley Novels*, rev. ed. (New Haven, Conn.: Yale University Press, 1968) to George Levine, *The Realistic Imagination* (Chicago: University of Chicago Press, 1981), emphasis falls on a distinct division in Scott between romance and "real history." Intelligent as this criticism is, Scott is not encompassed by it.

6. Fleishman's book is a great exception. Fleishman sees Scott "express . . . in fiction the organicist doctrines of Burke" (p. 55) and thereby prefigure Conrad. But the organicist Scott, for all his Burkeian surface, has a violent and radical streak that requires appreciation. For Scott's Polish influence, see Donald Davie, *The Heyday of Sir Walter Scott* (London: Routledge and Paul, 1961). I have elsewhere emphasized Conrad's close ties with Dickens ("Joseph Conrad, Dickensian Novelist of the Nineteenth Century: A Dissent from Ian Watt," in *Nineteenth Century Fiction* 36 (1981): 337–47; but close ties with Dickens are inevitably close ties with Scott. For Dickens's reliance on Scott see my *Plot, Story, and the Novel* (Princeton, N.J.: Princeton University Press, 1979), chapters 3 and 4.

Notes

7. The view I ascribe to Stevens is also to be found in Nelson Goodman, *Languages of Art* (New York: Harper and Row, 1968). My alternative formulation derives from Wollheim.

8. For stimulating my thoughts on an economy of representation I owe a debt to Kurt Heinzelman, *The Economics of the Imagination* (Amherst: University of Massachusetts Press, 1980). Heinzelman emphasizes an imaginative, literary version of labor theories of value. However, this emphasis may lead to the fabrications my focus on the category of the gift means to check.

9. My argument in this essay will have succeeded if it manages to complicate or qualify the leading biographical as well as critical studies of Conrad. Bernard C. Meyer, *Joseph Conrad: A Psychoanalytic Biography* (Princeton, N.J.: Princeton University Press, 1967), powerfully reduces the rescue theme in Conrad to neurotic symptomology; see chapter 7 especially. I hope I make Meyer's reduction somewhat less easy to maintain. Frederick Karl, *Joseph Conrad: The Three Lives* (New York: Farrar, Straus and Giroux, 1979), stresses Conrad's desire to be *modern* (see p. 468). But that this was a very divided desire is, in *The Rescue*'s light, I also hope more clear. Conrad's choice of an epigraph for *The Rescue* from Chaucer's Franklin's Tale does not show him pursuing modernity. In Chaucer's romance one finds many of *The Rescue*'s elements: among them, an artist-figure whose magic realism suggests Chaucer using the tale to dramatize his own art, and a sequence of ensnaring trades, fabrications, and debts that the artist-figure must cancel by means of a generous gift.

As this essay goes to press I discover Lewis Hyde, *The Gift* (New York: Random House, 1983). Hyde's theory of gifts and his "experiments in gift aesthetics" complement my views.

The Continuity of Conrad's Later Novels

Daniel R. Schwarz

1. From a February 6, 1918, letter to John Quinn; quoted in Frederick Karl, *Joseph Conrad: The Three Lives* (New York: Farrar, Straus and Giroux, 1979), pp. 807–8. I am indebted to Karl's account of Conrad's later years.

2. Quoted in ibid., p. 730, from a June 20, 1913, letter to Warrington Dawson.

3. For example, see an August 28, 1908, letter to Garnett; quoted in ibid., p. 650n.

4. Gérard Jean-Aubry, *Joseph Conrad: Life and Letters*, 2 vols. (Garden City, N.Y.: Doubleday, Page, 1927).

5. See Karl, *Joseph Conrad*, p. 639.

6. Bernard C. Meyer, *Joseph Conrad: A Psychoanalytic Biography* (Princeton, N.J.: Princeton University Press, 1967), p. 243.

7. Ibid., p. 221.

8. Thomas Moser, *Joseph Conrad: Achievement and Decline* (Cambridge, Mass.: Harvard University Press, 1957), p. 141.

9. Ibid., p. 140.

10. Ibid., p. 163.

11. See ibid., p. 144.

12. Ibid., p. 162.

13. Ibid., p. 180.

14. John Palmer, *Joseph Conrad's Fiction: A Study in Literary Growth* (Ithaca, N.Y.: Cornell University Press, 1968), pp. 168–69.

15. From an October 7, 1912, letter to Pinker; quoted in Karl, *Joseph Conrad*, p. 717.

16. From a December 8, 1912, letter to Edith Wharton; quoted and paraphrased in ibid., p. 725.

17. Page numbers in parentheses refer to the Kent edition (Garden City, N.Y.: Doubleday, Page, 1926).

18. In "Autocracy and War," Conrad had written: "The subtle and manifold influence for evil of the Napoleonic episode as a school of violence, as sower of national hatreds, as the direct provocator of obscurantism and reaction, of political tyranny and injustice, cannot well be exaggerated" (*Notes on Life and Letters*, p. 86).

Contributors

Robert Caserio is associate professor of English at Oberlin College. In addition to his book, entitled *Plot, Story, and the Novel*, he has published numerous essays on nineteenth- and twentieth-century American writing. He holds degrees from Columbia, Cambridge, and Yale universities and has taught at the State University of New York (Buffalo), at Columbia, and at Yale.

H. M. Daleski is professor of English at the Hebrew University of Jerusalem. He has published four books of criticism: *The Forked Flame: A Study of D. H. Lawrence, Dickens and the Art of Analogy, Joseph Conrad: The Way of Dispossession*, and *The Divided Heroine: A Recurrent Pattern in Six English Novels*. Professor Daleski was educated at the University of Witwatersand; Jesus College, Oxford; and the Hebrew University of Jerusalem. He has lived in Israel since the establishment of the state.

Avrom Fleishman is professor of English at The Johns Hopkins University. He has also taught at Minnesota, Michigan State, and Columbia. He is the author of *Conrad's Politics* and of works on the English historical novel, Jane Austen, Virginia Woolf, and Victorian and modern fiction. His major work, *Figures of Autobiography*, was published in 1983 by the University of California Press.

Contributors

Hunt Hawkins has published articles on Conrad in *PMLA*, *Conradiana*, *Joseph Conrad Today*, and the *Journal of Modern Literature*. His poems have appeared in *Poetry*, the *Carleton Miscellany*, *Harvard Magazine*, *Poetry Northwest*, and the *Beloit Poetry Journal*. A Stanford Ph.D., he has taught at Kurasini College in Tanzania, at Texas Southern University as a Woodrow Wilson Fellow, and at the University of Minnesota. He is currently assistant professor of English at Florida State University.

Bruce Johnson, the author of *Conrad's Models of Mind* and of numerous articles on Conrad and Hardy, is professor of English and chairman of the English department at the University of Rochester. Educated at the University of Chicago and at Northwestern University, he has been both an NEH Senior Fellow and a Guggenheim Fellow.

Frederick Karl is a professor of English at New York University. The author of *Joseph Conrad: The Three Lives* (a Pulitzer Prize finalist for biography in 1979), he is currently working on Conrad's *Letters*. Professor Karl has published extensively on the history of the English novel, with particular emphasis on Conrad and his contemporaries. He was educated at Columbia University and at Stanford University.

J. Hillis Miller was educated at Oberlin and at Harvard. He has taught at Williams College and The Johns Hopkins University, and is presently Frederick W. Hilles Professor of English and Comparative Literature at Yale University. One of the most versatile and provocative critics of our time, he is the author of such notable works as *Charles Dickens: The World of His Novels*, *The Disappearance of God*, *Thomas Hardy: Distance and Desire*, and, most recently, *Fiction and Repetition: Seven English Novels*.

Daniel R. Schwarz, professor of English at Cornell University, has published widely on nineteenth- and twentieth-century British literature. His books include *Disraeli's Fiction*, *Conrad: "Al-*

mayer's Folly" to "Under Western Eyes," and *Conrad: The Later Fiction.* He is currently working on a book tracing the development of the British novel from Hardy to Joyce.

Ross C Murfin, professor of English and Master of the Honors Residential College at the University of Miami, served as director of the Third International Joseph Conrad Conference. He came to Miami from Yale, where he was on the faculty for seven years. The author of *Swinburne, Hardy, Lawrence, and the Burden of Belief* and of *The Poetry of D. H. Lawrence: Texts and Contexts,* he is currently working on a study of the relationship between political, pictorial, and novelistic theories of representation.

Index

Index

Index